THE
HISTORY
OF
ISSUES

Hate Crimes

Other Books in the History of Issues Series:

Hate Crimes

Jennifer Bussey, Book Editor

GREENHAVEN PRESS
An imprint of Thomson Gale, a part of The Thomson Corporation

Detroit • New York • San Francisco • New Haven, Conn. • Waterville, Maine • London

Christine Nasso, *Publisher*
Elizabeth Des Chenes, *Managing Editor*

© 2007 The Gale Group.

Star logo is a trademark and Gale and Greenhaven Press are registered trademarks used herein under license.

For more information, contact:
Greenhaven Press
27500 Drake Rd.
Farmington Hills, MI 48331-3535
Or you can visit our Internet site at http://www.gale.com

Articles in Greenhaven Press anthologies are often edited for length to meet page requirements. In addition, original titles of these works are changed to clearly present the main thesis and to explicitly indicate the author's opinion. Every effort is made to ensure that Greenhaven Press accurately reflects the original intent of the authors. Every effort has been made to trace the owners of copyrighted material.

Cover photograph © Matthew McVay/Corbis.

LIBRARY OF CONGRESS CATALOGING-IN-PUBLICATION DATA

Hate crimes / Jennifer Bussey, book editor.
    p. cm. -- (History of issues)
Includes bibliographical references and index.
ISBN-13: 978-0-7377-2869-9 (hardcover)
1. Hate crimes--United States. 2. Hate groups--Government policy--United States.
3. Hate crimes--United States--Prevention. I. Bussey, Jennifer.
    HV6773.52.H363 2008
    364.15--dc22

                                                                    2007040010

ISBN-10: 0-7377-2869-8 (hardcover)

Printed in the United States of America
10 9 8 7 6 5 4 3 2 1

Contents

Chapter 2: Hate Groups and Anti-Hate Groups

The heightened security in the aftermath of 9/11 has led to profiling, increased airport security, limited rights, and talk of measures such as wiretaps and identity cards. Such compromises on human rights lead to a slippery slope that could result in great injustice against ethnic and religious groups.

Foreword

In the 1940s, at the height of the Holocaust, Jews struggled to create a nation of their own in Palestine, a region of the Middle East that at the time was controlled by Britain. The British had placed limits on Jewish immigration to Palestine, hampering efforts to provide refuge to Jews fleeing the Holocaust. In response to this and other British policies, an underground Jewish resistance group called Irgun began carrying out terrorist attacks against British targets in Palestine, including immigration, intelligence, and police offices. Most famously, the group bombed the King David Hotel in Jerusalem, the site of a British military headquarters. Although the British were warned well in advance of the attack, they failed to evacuate the building. As a result, ninety-one people were killed (including fifteen Jews) and forty-five were injured.

Early in the twentieth century, Ireland, which had long been under British rule, was split into two countries. The south, populated mostly by Catholics, eventually achieved independence and became the Republic of Ireland. Northern Ireland, mostly Protestant, remained under British control. Catholics in both the north and south opposed British control of the north, and the Irish Republican Army (IRA) sought unification of Ireland as an independent nation. In 1969, the IRA split into two factions. A new radical wing, the Provisional IRA, was created and soon undertook numerous terrorist bombings and killings throughout Northern Ireland, the Republic of Ireland, and even in England. One of its most notorious attacks was the 1974 bombing of a Birmingham, England, bar that killed nineteen people.

In the mid-1990s, an Islamic terrorist group called al Qaeda began carrying out terrorist attacks against American targets overseas. In communications to the media, the organization listed several complaints against the United States. It generally opposed all U.S. involvement and presence in the Middle East. It particularly objected to the presence of U.S. troops in Saudi Arabia, which is the home of several Islamic holy sites. And it strongly condemned the United States for supporting the nation of Israel, which it claimed was an oppressor of Muslims. In 1998 al Qaeda's leaders issued a fatwa (a religious legal statement) calling for Muslims to kill Americans. Al Qaeda acted on this order many times—most memorably on September 11, 2001, when it attacked the World Trade Center and the Pentagon, killing nearly three thousand people.

These three groups—Irgun, the Provisional IRA, and al Qaeda—have achieved varied results. Irgun's terror campaign contributed to Britain's decision to pull out of Palestine and to support the creation of Israel in 1948. The Provisional IRA's tactics kept pressure on the British, but they also alienated many would-be supporters of independence for Northern Ireland. Al Qaeda's attacks provoked a strong U.S. military response but did not lessen America's involvement in the Middle East nor weaken its support of Israel. Despite these different results, the means and goals of these groups were similar. Although they emerged in different parts of the world during different eras and in support of different causes, all three had one thing in common: They all used clandestine violence to undermine a government they deemed oppressive or illegitimate.

The destruction of oppressive governments is not the only goal of terrorism. For example, terror is also used to minimize dissent in totalitarian regimes and to promote extreme ideologies. However, throughout history the motivations of terrorists have been remarkably similar, proving the old adage that "the more things change, the more they remain the same." Arguments for and against terrorism thus boil down to the same set of universal arguments regardless of the age: Some argue that terrorism is justified to change (or, in the case of state terror, to maintain) the prevailing political order; others respond that terrorism is inhumane and unacceptable under any circumstances. These basic views transcend time and place.

Similar fundamental arguments apply to other controversial social issues. For instance, arguments over the death penalty have always featured competing views of justice. Scholars cite biblical texts to claim that a person who takes a life must forfeit his or her life, while others cite religious doctrine to support their view that only God can take a human life. These arguments have remained essentially the same throughout the centuries. Likewise, the debate over euthanasia has persisted throughout the history of Western civilization. Supporters argue that it is compassionate to end the suffering of the dying by hastening their impending death; opponents insist that it is society's duty to make the dying as comfortable as possible as death takes its natural course.

Greenhaven Press's History of Issues series illustrates this constancy of arguments surrounding major social issues. Each volume in the series focuses on one issue—including terrorism, the death penalty, and euthanasia—and examines how the debates have both evolved and remained essentially the same over the years. Primary documents such as newspaper articles, speeches, and government reports illuminate historical developments and offer perspectives from throughout history. Secondary sources provide overviews and commentaries from a more contemporary perspective. An introduction begins each anthology and supplies essential context and background. An annotated table of contents, chronology, and index allow for easy reference, and a bibliography and list of organizations to contact point to additional sources of information on the book's topic. With these features, History of Issues series permits readers to glimpse both the historical and contemporary dimensions of humanity's most pressing and controversial social issues.

Introduction

Hatred has always played a role in human interaction. For some, hatred toward particular groups is so intense that they organize violent efforts to lash out at those they hate. While much research has gone into what makes hate groups do what they do, it is also worthwhile to examine the ways hate victims respond collectively to being persecuted. At an individual level, victims respond in numerous ways—pressing charges, creating a public outcry, suffering silently, fighting back, and so on. But collectively, victim groups seem to respond in primarily two ways: some respond to hate and violence with more hate and violence, and some respond by persevering and using the system to seek protection and justice.

Human nature often compels people to respond to an attack with a counterattack, which may explain why so many victimized groups react to hate and violence with more of the same. Going on the offensive against an enemy brings a sense of strength and community. The history of hate crime in the United States is replete with examples of victimized groups responding in this way, from the early history of the nation to recent events. In the very early history of America, slavery was much more than an economic arrangement—it was a systematized way to exploit an entire race of people believed to be inferior. The history of slavery is the history of racial hatred and violence. Intimidation, threats, whippings, lynchings, rape, and humiliation were all used against slaves to render them powerless. Slave uprisings and revolts represented the slaves' passionate desire for freedom, but they were also violent demonstrations of the hate harbored by the slaves against their white oppressors. Slave uprisings have taken place in virtually every slave-holding society, which demonstrates that the response of hate and violence against hate and violence is a natural—and predictable—response. White slave owners were so afraid of uprisings that when they suspected rebellions were being planned, they responded with great force against the slaves.

Despite slave owners' attempts to prevent them, numerous slave uprisings were planned and many carried out. One of the first was the 1739 Stono Rebellion, led by a slave named Jemmy. After marching and shouting for liberty, the small group of rebels killed two shopkeepers and then set about burning the homes of slave owners. As they continued on their way, they gathered more slaves into their group, accumulating as many as 100 people by the end. A group of white men organized to stop them, and the ensuing fight cost the lives of 20 whites and 40 slaves. The participating slaves who were caught were beheaded. In 1800, a planned rebellion by Gabriel Prosser was suppressed when the owners caught wind of the plan. In response, they hanged Prosser and 25 others. Denmark Vesey planned a rebellion to take place on July 14, 1822. The rebellion involved close to 150 slaves, and the plan called for them to kill their masters and then escape as a group to Haiti. The masters learned of the plot, however, and charged 130 people with conspiracy, hanging 35 of them.

Less than ten years later, on August 21, 1831, the notorious Nat Turner rebellion took place. Turner and a small group of slaves traveled from farm to farm freeing slaves, and Turner encouraged them to kill the white families. As the number of slaves grew, the bloodshed intensified. By using quiet weapons instead of guns, the rebelling slaves made significant progress before a posse stopped them. All told, nearly sixty men, women, and children were slaughtered in the wake of the Nat Turner rebellion. In retaliation, fifty-five people were hanged for their involvement, while hundreds of others—involved or not—were beaten and punished for the rebellion. Turner himself evaded capture until late November, when he was captured and given a trial. Found guilty, he was sentenced to hang. The intense feelings involved in this situation were evidenced by the body count of the rebellion (which was less about escape than it was about lashing out against white oppression) and in the treatment of Turner's body after his execution. After he was hanged, his dead body was dismembered and parts given out as souvenirs.

The slave uprisings provide examples of how one group's hate and violence breeds the same in its victims, and thus the cycle perpetuates itself. Race relations between black and white Americans have been troubled throughout the nation's history and remain strained even today. Hate groups have emerged on both sides—white groups who hate blacks, and black groups who hate whites.

Another example of the cycle of hate and violence is in the early relations between settlers and Native Americans. European settlers believed that whatever lands they saw were theirs for the taking, disregarding the fact that Native Americans had been living on those lands for generations. Afraid of the natives, many settlers treated them violently, and some Native Americans responded in kind. Wars and massacres testify to the lengths to which the settlers and Native Americans went to fight for what they believed in. The Battle of Little Bighorn, which claimed the lives of over 250 American military personnel, is one example of a battle waged on American soil due to fundamental disagreements over what it means to live here, a battle between groups of people with little regard for each other. Among the most infamous altercations between whites and Native Americans was the massacre at Wounded Knee, South Dakota, which left about three hundred unarmed Lakota men, women, and children dead.

The events of September 11, 2001, showed the world the extent to which a radical hate group will go to devastate its target group and provided another tragic example of hate begetting hate. The people killed in the attacks on New York's World Trade Center and the Pentagon in Washington, D.C., and the passengers on United Airlines Flight 93, were all killed simply for being Americans. Because the attackers were of Arab descent, some Americans lashed out at innocent Arab Americans, who were as horrified by the attacks as anyone else. Jay Parini, an American who has traveled extensively throughout the Middle East for almost forty years, is now a frequent speaker at universities in Egypt and Jordan. He has seen how hate and violence not only affect interpersonal relations but also international affairs. In a 2006 *Commonweal* article titled "An American in Egypt: No Longer an Innocent Abroad," he writes, "I always say firmly to my audience and anyone who will listen, that violence is not an appropriate response to violence, as it merely continues a cycle that becomes difficult to break."

A second collective response to hate and violence is perseverance, using the system to seek justice and protection. Treatment of early Chinese settlers in the United States was often motivated by bigotry. Although they had come to America to work hard to support their families in the land of opportunity, the Chinese were misunderstood, mocked, and abused. Rather than mobilize so they could fight violence with violence, early Chinese immigrants stood their ground as best they could and persevered under the weight of mistreatment. Eventually, the system extended protections to them, and they were able to establish themselves in their adopted nation.

The perseverance response is personified by Martin Luther King Jr., whose dominant role in the civil rights movement was as a leader who called for peaceful resolution to nonpeaceful problems. King certainly understood the tendency to respond to hate with hate, but he believed that the solution lay in rising above human nature. In 1958 he explained, "Hate begets hate. Violence begets violence. Toughness begets a greater toughness. We must meet the forces of hate with the power of love." He added, "Our aim must never be to defeat or humiliate the white man, but to win his friendship and understanding." Nonviolent protests and efforts to change the laws and policies of local, state, and federal governments were his tools, and he used them effectively. Unlike some of his peers, King believed that if African Americans conducted themselves with dignity, rose above their struggles, and pursued equality through unity, they would achieve fair and equal treatment. Across America, thousands of people followed him and organized their efforts according to his principles.

King's message of nonviolence was difficult for many of his followers to embrace when on April 4, 1968, he was assassinated by James Earl Ray. Ironically, King's death set off riots all over the nation. But his lessons were not completely forgotten. The racially motivated murders of Michael Griffith and Yusuf Hawkins in New York in the 1980s inspired members of the African American community to mobilize and demonstrate against hate crimes. In fact, the New York Civil Rights Coalition was formed after Griffith's murder and was then able to step in on Hawkins's behalf to help prosecute the case and seek justice. The result of the demonstrations and the cases was public condemnation of the perpetrators who had carried out their violence in private. Many New Yorkers thus saw more clearly how deep the problem of racism went in their city.

Among the most recent examples of the activist response to hatred has been from the gay and lesbian community. While this group has been targeted for many generations, recent decades have seen a rise in crimes against its members primarily due to their increased visibility and openness. Individuals and groups who hate gays and lesbians are threatened by this growing presence and acceptance in American culture, so they lash out verbally and physically. There have been a number of high-profile hate crimes against gays, lesbians, and transgendered persons, with victims including Billy Jack Gaither, Rashawn Brazell, J. R. Warren, Matthew Shepard, Sakia Gunn, and Gwen Araujo. Gay and lesbian groups have largely adopted nonviolent ways to retaliate and protect their members.

Through protests, petition campaigns, lobbying, organizing crisis and victim assistance, and promoting education, they have sought to shed light on their situation and garner support from within and without their groups. The gay, lesbian, and transgendered communities have chosen activism as their primary weapon against hate crime and bigotry.

When victimized groups seek to empower themselves through legal or public organizations, they often face further targeting by those who hate them. In her book *Understanding Hate Crimes* (2001), Barbara Perry explains, "Paradoxically, efforts to render minority communities impotent—whether through the mechanism of hate crime or other repressive means—can backfire. Rather than hobbling the victim group, they may in fact mobilize the community. . . . Unfortunately, this posture of empowerment often is seen as an affront to white dominance. The victim community is perceived to be violating the anticipated rules of behavior. Instead of accepting their subordination, they resist it." A similar attitude was seen in the response to slavery and in the slave owners' response to uprisings. In both cases, one group fights back against another's efforts to assert itself.

Whether a group responds by answering hate with more hate or by nonviolent means, the collective response is far more visible and influential than an individual response. While even the most powerful group response will probably not bring an end to hate crimes against members of that group, such responses can have tremendous impact on society.

CHAPTER 1

Hate Crimes in History

Chapter Preface

Instances of people lashing out in hate have plagued humankind throughout history. Perhaps the most horrifying example of widespread violence motivated by hate was the Holocaust during World War II by Adolf Hitler's Nazi Germany. Beginning with discriminatory policies and escalating to imprisonment and systematic murder, the Holocaust resulted in the deaths of millions of innocent people. An estimated six million Jews were killed, in addition to an estimated five million people singled out for their politics, religion, ethnicity, disability, or sexual orientation. Hitler harbored a deep and abiding hatred for and distrust of those he considered inferior, and he brought all his power, influence, and intimidation to bear on eliminating such groups of people from the world. He sought to control the population and become the great designer of what he described as a master race, a superior breed of people. His hatred moved him and his officers to be exceedingly cold and brutal, dehumanizing their victims as part of their plan to commit genocide. Survivor accounts provide a deeply disturbing picture of the human devastation wrought by Hitler and his followers.

Also disturbing are instances of racial violence throughout American history. As racial tensions came to a head during the 1950s and 1960s, groups on both sides mobilized to take action. Particularly in the South, the white reaction to the growing African American civil rights movement was often violent and even murderous. Discrimination, offensive language, threats, and vandalism were common, but the news also carried stories about beatings and bombings. One of the most notorious bombings was of the Sixteenth Street Baptist Church in Birmingham, Alabama. The city was a hotbed of racial tension and had seen so many bombings from the late 1940s through the mid-1960s that it became known as "Bombingham." In the wake of a court decision to integrate schools, a group of segregationists decided to protest by setting off a bomb in a black church. On the morning of September 15, 1963, four black girls—Denise McNair, Carole Robertson, Cynthia Wesley, and Addie Mae Collins—sat preparing for Sunday School in the basement of the church when the bomb exploded, killing all four of them. The event set off a wave of racial violence that spread throughout the city. Unfortunately, city officials were not very interested in bringing the bombers to justice; it was not until fourteen years later that even one of the perpetrators was convicted.

Hate violence has been manifested around the world on every possible scale, from Hitler's plan to destroy European Jewry to a segregationist group's targeting of a small American church, to everything in between. Regardless of changes made in modern societies—laws to prevent discrimination and to harshen punishments for hate crimes, as well as an increasing acceptance of diversity—hate crimes continue to be a blight on American society and throughout the world.

Hate Has Always Motivated Violence and Discrimination Around the World

Jack Levin and Jack McDevitt

The issue of hate crimes is not limited to a single nation or a particular time period. Hate crimes plague nations around the world, even in modern times when there is so much emphasis on tolerance. Today, countries as different from each other as China, Italy, and Hungary face the difficulties associated with racial, religious, and ethnic tensions that often lead to violence. Tensions have a tendency to come to a head when a country undergoes a period of change in economic, political, or social structure. In the following viewpoint, Jack Levin and Jack McDevitt examine the ways hate groups respond to change by attacking people they perceive as threatening, unworthy, or inferior. Levin is a professor of sociology and criminology at Northeastern University, where he also serves as the director of the Brudnick Center on Conflict and Violence. He is the author or coauthor of more than twenty books and has written more than 150 articles for journals and newspapers. McDevitt is a criminologist and associate director of the Center for Applied Research at Northeastern University. He and Levin cowrote Hate Crimes Revisited: America's War on Those Who Are Different.

The voices of xenophobia and racism are once again reverberating throughout German society. The resentment associated with hate crimes can be clearly seen in a sweeping new wave of violence—the largest spree of racial violence in Germany since the early days of Nazism.

Jack Levin and Jack McDevitt, *Hate Crimes: The Rising Tide of Bigotry and Bloodshed.* New York: Westview Press, 2001, pp. 149–58. Copyright © 1993 Jack Levin and Jack McDevitt. Reprinted by permission of Basic Books, a member of Perseus Books Group.

Recent changes in what used to be East Germany as it struggles to make the transition from a communist to a freemarket economy have set the stage for violent attacks on refugees and workers from Eastern European and Third World countries. Unemployment has approached 50 percent in some eastern cities, and the collapse of the once tightly controlled communist economic system has made living conditions deplorable. There is a housing shortfall in the major cities. Young Germans watch as their parents lose their jobs, their teachers are replaced, and their old political heroes are arrested. According to Heinrich Sosalla, director of social services in Magdeburg, "young people are desperate for some sort of new authority." Some find it in a revised version of Nazi activism; they work out their frustrations on a new scapegoat—the hundreds of thousands of foreign refugees who struggle to gain a foothold in their host country.

Five million foreigners reside in Germany, including hundreds of thousands who seek political asylum and almost three million "guest workers"—émigrés who are permitted to reside in Germany because they are needed to fill a particular job—and their families, most of whom are permanently excluded from citizenship. In addition, about 400,000 ethnic Germans in the Soviet Union—persons of German ancestry—who return to the fatherland are automatically granted citizenship.

The contributions of newcomers to a thriving German economy should not be underestimated. They provide a cheap source of labor that keeps industry competitive, spurs investments, and revitalizes decaying communities. Many of them perform jobs that native-born Germans see as simply beneath them. Moreover, the population of Western Europe is waning and aging rapidly. The presence of large numbers of immigrants assures that Germany will be able to maintain its current labor force.

Neo-Nazi Groups Turn Violent

All of this is lost on the hordes of out-of-work neo-Nazi German youths who regard newcomers as little more than insects to be crushed under foot. During 1991 alone, there were almost 1,500 attacks against foreigners in Germany, but only a handful of convictions. In April 1991, a twenty-eight-year-old Mozambican was killed by a gang of East German neo-Nazi youths who pushed him from a moving trolley in the city of Dresden. In September 1991, 600 right-wing German youths firebombed a home for foreigners and then physically assaulted 200 Vietnamese and Mozambicans in the streets of Hoyerswerde.

More recently, normal tranquility in the East German seaport town of Rostock was shattered by seven nights of organized violence in the streets. Armed with gasoline bombs and stones, a thousand Nazi youths attempted to force out foreigners seeking asylum in Germany. First, the mob firebombed a ten-story hostel in which Romanian gypsies were housed. Then, they stormed the building next door, a residence for Vietnamese "guest workers," and set it on fire. Some 600 police officers in riot gear used water cannons and tear gas to subdue the crowd. At least 195 Nazi youths were arrested. One hundred and fifteen Vietnamese and 200 Romanians were evacuated by police and relocated to a former East German army barracks under heavy guard. Within days, the attacks in Rostock had touched off a massive wave of antiforeign violence in at least twenty cities around eastern Germany.

Extremists Are Few, but Sympathizers Are Many

Much of the violence in Germany is perpetrated by a relatively small number of extremists—an estimated 5,000 hardcore neo-Nazis and another 30,000 racist skinheads out of a total German population of almost 78 million. In East Berlin, a chapter of neo-Nazis recruited only a few hundred unemployed and alienated young men who give expression to bigotry and racism as a way of "fighting back." Several hundred neo-Nazis from former East German towns recently met to commemorate the death of Hitler's deputy Rudolf Hess.

Yet, the degree of resentment can be easily underestimated. There are actually millions of "silent sympathizers." In a recent national poll, up to 40 percent of all Germans expressed some sympathy for the issues—"Germany for Germans," "racial purity," and "foreigners out"—espoused by right-wing extremists. Moreover, 15 percent of Germany's youth said they now consider Adolf Hitler to have been a great man. In Germany and surrounding European countries, violence is taught by means of underground Nazi computer games, which have recently circulated among high school students there. In the game "Aryan Test," players are asked to indicate the most effective method for exterminating Jews. The winning answer is to kill them in gas chambers. In the game "Concentration Camp Manager," the objective is to kill as many Turks with as little gas as possible.

Racial Tension in China Leads to Persecution

Even in China, where foreigners have long enjoyed deferential treatment, there are signs that resentment against the 1,500 African students who study there has been on the rise. Former minor points of contention have become major points of conflict. In 1989, two black African students showed up with their Chinese dates to attend a Christmas Eve dance in the city of Nanjing. Word of this incident spread quickly, precipitating several racially motivated confrontations between college students. Hearing about the demonstrations in Nanjing, young people in several other Chinese cities met en masse to express their collective displeasure with the foreigners. Thousands of demonstrators screamed racial slogans like "Beat the blacks." Rather than deal harshly with the local students who rioted, the police in Nanjing instead beat the African students, held them incommunicado, and even tortured them by shocking them on the genitals with cattle prods.

The Chinese are apparently resentful of a historical tendency, probably motivated by politics, for foreigners to be given special treatment by China's government. On trains, for example, Chinese passengers travel "hard class," while foreigners and high officials ride in the "soft class" cars. Similarly, Chinese students on university campuses see their government furnishing African students with special dormitories, cafeterias, and scholarships. Thus, African students are particularly resented not only because of simple racism, but because these foreigners are seen as getting preferential treatment.

Anti-Muslim and Anti-Jewish Hatred in France

In France, mounting resentment against its three million Muslim Arab immigrants has provoked the government to tighten controls against illegal immigration. Public opinion pollsters report that 76 percent of all French citizens now believe that there are too many Arabs in their country. Jean-Marie Le Pen's extreme right-wing National Front, a powerful political force in some regions of France, has called for the eviction of all immigrants. Le Pen has made his greatest inroads in areas of France having high unemployment and large immigrant communities. In the port city of Marseilles, the home of many North African newcomers for example, the sixty-three-year-old Le Pen recently won 25 percent of the vote. In some cases, anti-immigrant sentiment has been transformed into ugly acts of violence. In March 1990, three men of North African origin were viciously murdered in separate racially motivated attacks.

Le Pen's anti-immigrant position is matched in fervor only by his anti-Semitism. He has openly disputed the authenticity of the Holocaust, dismissing stories of Nazi gas chambers as "historical detail," and has often raised the issue of national loyalty among French Jews. In a widely shown television debate, Le Pen repeatedly asked Lionel Stoleru, a Jewish government minister, whether he held both Israeli and French citizenship. "We have the right to know who you are," Le Pen told Stoleru.

Perhaps inspired by its right-wing political movement, France has also been forced to deal with a rising tide of crimes against Jews. Through the 1980s and into the 1990s, numerous Jewish cemeteries have been vandalized. In May 1990, a particularly grisly series of desecrations occurred. At the cemetery in Carpentras, situated in southern France, vandals shattered thirty-four tombstones with sledgehammers and iron bars. They then dragged one woman's body halfway out of her grave and exhumed the body of an eighty-one-year-old man buried only two weeks earlier. As an expression of their disdain, the vandals impaled the man in the middle of his chest with an umbrella to hold in place a Star of David.

Violence Against Immigrants in Italy

In Italy, a traditional haven for newcomers, hospitality has similarly turned cold, as the Italian economy worsens, unemployment grows, and the influx of newcomers remains unchecked. Hardly a week passes without some episode of conflict between immigrants and Italians. In March 1990, for example, a large gang of Florentine youths battered their way into an immigrant dormitory and beat up immigrant workers. In May 1991, a crowd of Italians cheered as the police arrested a group of Albanians who were demonstrating in the city of Asti to protest the living conditions in their refugee camp. Also in May 1991, two Italian workers placed a high-powered air-compression hose into a Moroccan coworker's anus, destroying his intestines and killing him.

There are some 800,000 legal immigrants in Italy, many of whom hold jobs as domestics and physical laborers. Some Italians argue that, given their country's very low birth rate, immigrants are necessary to the vitality of the economy. But most Italians see the high unemployment rate and argue instead that immigrants are taking their jobs. In fact, 75 percent of all Italians now favor closing the borders to all new immigration.

Eastern European Racism and Anti-Semitism

As the economic woes in Eastern Europe have worsened, racism and anti-Semitism have resurged. In Moscow, twenty-five-year-old Zimbabwean student Gideon Chimusoro was fatally shot in the neck by police after he kicked a dog belonging to the owner of a kiosk. When Chimusoro's classmates marched in protest, riot troops clubbed and kicked them to the ground. Some of the African students were pinned against walls and pounded viciously with clubs. Dozens of Russian onlookers, disgusted by the sight of protesting Africans, made obscene gestures at the demonstrators. All of the students attended classes at Moscow's Patrice Lumumba People's Friendship University, once a showcase of communist propaganda but now a run-down institution beset with charges of neglect and racism.

In what was formerly the Soviet Union, political factions have focused their assault on the small Jewish minority in an effort to force Jews to give up good jobs or to leave the country. Hundreds of thousands have already left; millions more are on their way out. Procommunist groups have used Jews as scapegoats to explain the demise of Soviet Marxism; anticommunists have blamed Jews for the current state of economic misery. In February 1992, anti-Semites marched through the streets of Moscow, shouting "Beat the Yids and save Russia" and demanding the dismissal of Jews from important public positions.

Given the minuscule number of its Jewish citizens, the growing anti-Semitic impulse in Poland seems particularly absurd. In a country of 38 million, there are now fewer than

10,000 Jews, most of whom are in their eighties. Yet, this fact hasn't diminished the public debate concerning whether or not public officials ought to be required to reveal their Jewish ancestry. Scrawled across Jewish monuments, graffiti hoping to discredit popular Polish figures make false claims that they are actually secret Jews.

The 80,000 Jews in Hungary have similarly experienced a revival of anti-Semitic sentiment, at the same time that they benefit from a rising tide of democracy. Just as in other countries of Eastern Europe, the demolition of the Soviet Union has made possible a new degree of Jewish practice unthinkable under the communist order. Hungary has resumed relations with Israel. The central synagogue in Budapest is now filled to capacity on religious holidays. An official memorial to the country's Holocaust victims was recently dedicated. And the first Jewish secular school is in full operation.

Anti-Semitism in Hungarian Politics

Yet, because some Jews held party positions under the communist system, the new Hungarian version of anti-Semitism is being merged with anticommunism. During the national election in 1990, for example, Miklos Tamas, an important member of the Hungarian Parliament, was singled out for harassment. While Tamas's political party is avowedly anticommunist, it appeals to a broad constituency, including many intellectuals, former communists, and Jews. A practicing Protestant whose mother was Jewish, Tamas received at least thirty anti-Semitic death threats by mail and telephone. In one letter, the anonymous bigot wrote, "The place for the Jews is Israel; the place for Dr. Tamas is the cemetery."

During the election campaign, one Hungarian political party sought to exploit anti-Semitism by making veiled references in its radio broadcasts to the "dwarfish minority" that was stealing Hungarian culture from its people. In an article published in the Hungarian socialist press, Jews were told that they must limit their presence in visible occupations—for example, in radio, TV, and newspapers—in order to assure that anti-Semitism would not increase. The socialist columnist Gyorgy Domokos wrote, "They must be careful that the number of Jews does not dominate."

Paul Bookbinder, Professor of History at the University of Massachusetts in Boston, suggests that the old Soviet regime—by means of police state tactics and extremely tight controls—had long suppressed overt expressions of anti-Semitism. According to Bookbinder, "anti-Semitism had no place officially in communist ideology and, in fact, was specifically opposed by early creators of the communist movement. From 1919 through the 1930s, anti-Semitism was against the law in the Soviet Union, and people were prosecuted for distributing anti-Semitic propaganda or committing acts of violence against Jews."

Bookbinder contends that the Russian government was generally passive in its reaction to bigotry. If it seldom singled out Jews for harassment, then the Soviet system did even less to attack the centuries-long underlying roots of anti-Semitism. Under communism, bigotry lay dormant but never disappeared, instead festering among many elements of the population. In the wake of the disintegration of the Soviet Union, Eastern Europeans were free for the first time since the Russian Revolution to express their beliefs and feelings openly. Thus, when the tight controls were lifted, anti-Semitism burst loose with a vengeance.

Origins and Purposes of Hate Crimes Around the World

To some extent, violence directed against newcomers may reflect an almost constant mixture of such irrational factors as racism, ethnocentrism, and xenophobia. Regardless of the state of the economy at any given point in history, certain members of society—especially those who can trace their own ancestry in a country back several generations—are bound to be offended by, and seek to remove, the strange customs, rituals, and appearance of "inferior outsiders."

At the same time, however, anti-immigrant and anti-Semitic violence also may have a more "rational" political and economic basis. During periods of economic retrenchment, it sends a powerful message to foreigners and minorities from those who seek to reduce competition for jobs. Hate violence says to anyone considering emigrating for the sake of a better standard of living: "Your kind is not welcome in *our* country. Don't bother to come. If you do, the same thing will happen to *you*." And to minorities, it says loud and clear: "Go back where you came from . . . or else."

As a form of collective scapegoating, hate violence serves a purpose for the rulers of a nation as well. Sociologist Lewis Coser once referred to this phenomenon as a "safety valve." He suggested that when times are bad, hostility that might otherwise be directed at the leaders of a society is instead aimed squarely at its marginal members, those located along the bottom-most rungs of the socioeconomic ladder. Thus, by focusing blame on the "outsiders," the rulers of a society are able to preserve their positions of power, even if their policies and programs are in fact responsible for pervasive economic hardships.

Not unlike other countries around the world, the United States has been guilty of using hate violence as a "safety valve" when times are tough. According to Jorge Bustamante, the president of El Colegio de la Frontera Norte in Tijuana, Mexico, it invariably becomes politically correct to capitalize on anti-immigrant sentiments whenever the U.S. unemployment rate rises above politically acceptable levels. When Americans are out of work, we can expect to hear our public officials call for repatriating recent arrivals, establishing more stringent criteria for accepting refugees, and closing the borders with Mexico. This is when immigrants are routinely blamed for Americans being out of work, for trafficking in drugs, for increasing the cost of social services, and for committing violent crime.

The Massacre of Native Americans at Wounded Knee

Dee Brown

The treatment of Native Americans by early American settlers and their government remains a source of shame in U.S. history. Stripped of their land, refused basic rights, and warred against, Native Americans were victimized on virtually every level. The attitude that accompanied (and motivated) such treatment made some people in power feel that they could do whatever they liked when it came to Indians. One of the most infamous examples of this was the massacre of Lakota men, women, and children at Wounded Knee in late December 1890. Author and historian Dee Brown made his reputation with his book Bury My Heart at Wounded Knee. *The book chronicles the history of the destruction of Native Americans under the motto "the only good Indian is a dead Indian." No event illustrates this attitude more clearly than the massacre at Wounded Knee. What follows is Brown's historical account of that day.*

Death of Sioux Chief

Had it not been for the sustaining force of the Ghost Dance religion, the Sioux in their grief and anger over the assassination of Sitting Bull [on December 15, 1890,] might have risen up against the guns of the soldiers. So prevalent was their belief that the white men would soon disappear and that with the next greening of the grass their dead relatives and friends would return, they made no retaliations. By the hundreds, however, the leaderless Hunkpapas fled from Standing Rock, seeking refuge in one of the Ghost Dance camps or with the last of the great chiefs, Red Cloud, at Pine Ridge. In the Moon

Dee Brown, *Bury My Heart at Wounded Knee*. New York: Henry Holt and Company, LLC, 1970. Copyright © 1970 by Dee Brown. All rights reserved. Reproduced by permission of Henry Holt and Company, LLC.

When the Deer Shed Their Horns (December 17 [1890]) about a hundred of these fleeing Hunkpapas reached Big Foot's Minneconjou camp near Cherry Creek. That same day the [U.S.] War Department issued orders for the arrest and imprisonment of Big Foot. He was on the list of "fomenters of disturbances."

As soon as Big Foot learned that Sitting Bull had been killed, he started his people toward Pine Ridge, hoping that Red Cloud could protect them from the soldiers. En route, he fell ill of pneumonia, and when hemorrhaging began, he had to travel in a wagon. On December 28, as they neared Porcupine Creek, the Minneconjous sighted four troops of cavalry approaching. Big Foot immediately ordered a white flag run up over his wagon. About two o'clock in the afternoon he raised up from his blankets to greet Major Samuel Whitside, Seventh U.S. Cavalry. Big Foot's blankets were stained with blood from his lungs, and as he talked in a hoarse whisper with Whitside, red drops fell from his nose and froze in the bitter cold.

Orders to Go to Wounded Knee

Whitside told Big Foot that he had orders to take him to a cavalry camp on Wounded Knee Creek. The Minneconjou chief replied that he was going in that direction; he was taking his people to Pine Ridge for safety.

Turning to his half-breed scout, John Shangreau, Major Whitside ordered him to begin disarming Big Foot's band.

"Look here, Major," Shangreau replied, "if you do that, there is liable to be a fight here; and if there is, you will kill all those women and children and the men will get away from you."

Whitside insisted that his orders were to capture Big Foot's Indians and disarm and dismount them.

"We better take them to camp and then take their horses from them and their guns," Shangreau declared.

"All right," Whitside agreed. "You tell Big Foot to move down to camp at Wounded Knee."

The major glanced at the ailing chief, and then gave an order for his Army ambulance to be brought forward. The ambulance would be warmer and would give Big Foot an easier ride than the jolting, springless wagon. After the chief was transferred to the ambulance, Whitside formed a column for the march to Wounded Knee Creek. Two troops of cavalry took the lead, the ambulance and wagons following, the Indians herded into a compact group behind them, with the other two cavalry troops and a battery of two Hotchkiss guns bringing up the rear.

Approaching Wounded Knee

Twilight was falling when the column crawled over the last rise in the land and began descending the slope toward Chankpe Opi Wakpala, the creek called Wounded Knee. The wintry dusk and the tiny crystals of ice dancing in the dying light added a supernatural quality to the somber landscape. Somewhere along this frozen stream the heart of Crazy Horse lay in a secret place, and the Ghost Dancers believed that his disembodied spirit was waiting impatiently for the new earth that would surely come with the first green grass of spring.

At the cavalry tent camp on Wounded Knee Creek, the Indians were halted and carefully counted. There were 120 men and 230 women and children. Because of the gathering darkness, Major Whitside decided to wait until morning before disarming his prisoners. He assigned them a camping area immediately to the south of the military camp, issued them rations, and as there was a shortage of tepee covers, he furnished them several tents. Whitside ordered a stove placed in Big Foot's tent and sent a regimental surgeon to administer to the sick chief. To make certain that none of his prisoners escaped, the major stationed two troops of cavalry as sentinels around the Sioux tepees, and then posted his two Hotchkiss guns on top of a rise overlooking the camp. The barrels of these rifled guns, which could hurl explosive charges for more than two miles, were positioned to rake the length of the Indian lodges.

Change of Army Command to Forsyth

Later in the darkness of that December night the remainder of the Seventh Regiment marched in from the east and quietly bivouacked north of Major Whitside's troops. Colonel James W. Forsyth, commanding Custer's former regiment, now took charge of operations. He informed Whitside that he had received orders to take Big Foot's band to the Union Pacific Railroad for shipment to a military prison in Omaha.

After placing two more Hotchkiss guns on the slope beside the others, Forsyth and his officers settled down for the evening with a keg of whiskey to celebrate the capture of Big Foot.

The chief lay in his tent, too ill to sleep, barely able to breathe. Even with their protective Ghost Shirts and their belief in the prophecies of the new Messiah, his people were fearful of the pony soldiers camped all around them. Fourteen years before, on the Little Bighorn, some of these warriors had helped defeat some of these soldier chiefs—Moylan, Varnum, Wallace, Godfrey, Edgerly—and the Indians wondered if revenge could still be in their hearts.

"The following morning there was a bugle call," said Wasumaza, one of Big Foot's warriors who years afterward was to change his name to Dewey Beard. "Then I saw the soldiers mounting their horses and surrounding us. It was announced that all men should come to the center for a talk and that after the talk they were to move on to Pine Ridge agency. Big Foot was brought out of his tepee and sat in front of his tent and the older men were gathered around him and sitting right near him in the center."

Disarming the Sioux

After issuing hardtack for breakfast rations, Colonel Forsyth informed the Indians that they were now to be disarmed. "They called for guns and arms," White Lance said, "so all of us gave the guns and they were stacked up in the center." The soldier chiefs were not satisfied with the number of weapons surrendered, and so they sent details of troopers to search the tepees. "They would go right into the tents and come out with bundles and tear them open," Dog Chief said. "They brought our axes, knives, and tent stakes and piled them near the guns."

Still not satisfied, the soldier chiefs ordered the warriors to remove their blankets and submit to searches for weapons. The Indians' faces showed their anger, but only the medicine man, Yellow Bird, made any overt protest. He danced a few Ghost Dance steps, and chanted one of the holy songs, assuring the warriors that the soldiers' bullets could not penetrate their sacred garments. "The bullets will not go toward you," he chanted in Sioux. "The prairie is large and the bullets will not go toward you."

The troopers found only two rifles, one of them a new Winchester belonging to a young Minneconjou named Black Coyote. Black Coyote raised the Winchester above his head, shouting that he paid much money for the rifle and that it belonged to him. Some years afterward Dewey Beard recalled that Black Coyote was deaf. "If they had left him alone he was going to put his gun down where he should. They grabbed him and spinned him in the east direction. He was still unconcerned even then. He hadn't his gun pointed at anyone. His intention was to put that gun down. They came on and grabbed the gun that he was going to put down. Right after they spun him around there was the report of a gun; was quite loud. I couldn't say that anybody was shot, but following that was a crash."

The Massacre Begins

"It sounded much like the sound of tearing canvas, that was the crash," Rough Feather said. Afraid-of-the-Enemy described it as a "lightning crash."

Turning Hawk said that Black Coyote "was a crazy man, a young man of very bad influence and in fact a nobody." He said that Black Coyote fired his gun and that "immediately the soldiers returned fire and indiscriminate killing followed."

In the first seconds of violence, the firing of carbines was deafening, filling the air with powder smoke. Among the dying who lay sprawled on the frozen ground was Big Foot. Then there was a brief lull in the rattle of arms, with small groups of Indians and soldiers grappling at close quarters, using knives, clubs, and pistols. As few of the Indians had arms, they soon had to flee, and then the big Hotchkiss guns on the hill opened up on them, firing almost a shell a second, raking the Indian camp, shredding the tepees with flying shrapnel, killing men, women, and children.

"We tried to run," Louise Weasel Bear said, "but they shot us like we were a buffalo. I know there are some good white people, but the soldiers must be mean to shoot children and women. Indian soldiers would not do that to white children."

"I was running away from the place and followed those who were running away," said Hakiktawin, another of the young women. "My grandfather and grandmother and brother were killed as we crossed the ravine, and then I was shot on the right hip clear through and on my right wrist where I did not go any further as I was not able to walk, and after the soldier picked me up where a little girl came to me and crawled into the blanket."

When the madness ended, Big Foot and more than half of his people were dead or seriously wounded; 153 were known dead, but many of the wounded crawled away to die afterward. One estimate placed the final total of dead at very nearly three hundred of the original 350 men, women, and children.

The soldiers lost twenty-five dead and thirty-nine wounded, most of them struck by their own bullets or shrapnel.

Aftermath

After the wounded cavalrymen were started for the agency at Pine Ridge, a detail of soldiers went over the Wounded Knee battlefield, gathering up Indians who were still alive and loading them into wagons. As it was apparent by the end of the day that a blizzard was approaching, the dead Indians were left lying where they had fallen. (After the blizzard, when a burial party returned to Wounded Knee, they found the bodies, including Big Foot's, frozen into grotesque shapes.)

The wagonloads of wounded Sioux (four men and forty-seven women and children) reached Pine Ridge after dark. Because all available barracks were filled with soldiers, they were left lying in the open wagons in the bitter cold while an inept Army officer searched for shelter. Finally the Episcopal mission was opened, the benches taken out, and hay scattered over the rough flooring.

It was the fourth day after Christmas in the Year of Our Lord 1890. When the first torn and bleeding bodies were carried into the candlelit church, those who were conscious could see Christmas greenery hanging from the open rafters. Across the chancel front above the pulpit was strung a crudely lettered banner: PEACE ON EARTH, GOOD WILL TO MEN.

Ida B. Wells's Campaigns Against Lynching in the American South

Patricia A. Schechter

Lynching was used in the American South to "punish" African Americans (usually men) and to keep the balance of power in favor of the whites. Lynching generally consisted of a group of white men taking a victim, beating him severely, and then hanging him. This was to serve not only as so-called justice but also as a warning to others. The practice of lynching carried strong racial and gender elements, and women recognized what was at stake for their race and its future. It was women who ultimately formed the antilynching movement, and Ida B. Wells was a pioneer in this area. She became an outspoken and strong opponent of lynching, effecting social change and setting an example for other African American women. In the following viewpoint, Patricia A. Schechter reviews the use of lynching in the late nineteenth century and chronicles Wells's rise to prominence in speaking out against it. Schechter is the author of Ida B. Wells-Barnett and American Reform, 1880–1930. *She is an associate professor of history at Portland State University in Oregon.*

In the late nineteenth- and early twentieth-century American South, lynching ended thousands of lives and politicized gender across and within racial lines. The archetypal "lynching story" reported in mainstream newspapers justified lynching as punishment for black men's alleged sexual assaults on white women. These accounts portrayed white males as patriarchal protectors of white females against African American men, the so-called black beasts or burly brutes who functioned as dark

Patricia A. Schechter, "Unsettled Business: Ida B. Wells against Lynching, or, How Antilynching Got Its Gender," *Under Sentence of Death: Lynching in the South*, Chapel Hill: University of North Carolina Press, 1997, pp. 292–317.

foils for true (white) manhood. White women appeared as passive, dependent, usually silent victims. This conventional story, for all its drama, left out the white women, black women, and white men who were also historical victims of lynching and ignored the active role of white women in abetting or resisting mobs. Furthermore, black women were totally invisible in the dominant lynching story. Yet middle-class black women, led by Ida B. Wells in the early 1890s, became lynching's most articulate and daring public critics. . . .

Though not recognized by scholars until recently, Wells's first published pamphlet, *Southern Horrors: Lynch Law in All Its Phases* (1892), is a point of origin in American critical thought on lynching. Wells's brief but comprehensive account offered a stinging critique of southern society as a "white man's country." After identifying lynching as a chief expression of "opposition . . . to the progress of the race," Wells made a creative new analysis of sex-race politics that owed little ideological debt to maternalism or the rhetoric of womanhood typical of nineteenth-century women's writing. Wells's reports of consensual and sometimes illicit sexual contact between white women and black men and of white women's role in abetting mobs undermined the assumption of white women's moral purity used to justify lynching. Furthermore, Wells probed the politics of "true manhood" in the lynching story and linked black men's oppression through lynching to black women's oppression through rape. Finally, her exploration and reworking of racial and sexual ideology claimed new authority for black women with the goal "that justice be done though the heavens fall. . . ."

During the 1880s, Memphis, Tennessee, where Ida B. Wells lived and worked as a teacher and journalist, was home to a thriving black community. Hoping to make Memphis the "Chicago of the South," city boosters fostered development with a degree of racial tolerance. But as black Memphians tried to turn progress into equality, white resistance appeared.

In 1883, for example, Wells brought a suit against a railroad company that refused to honor her ticket for a seat in a first-class car after the trainman roughly, forcibly removed her from the car. No major racial violence occurred in Memphis—the site of the post–Civil War South's bloodiest race riot in 1866—until 1892, when three black shopkeepers were lynched because they posed an unacceptable economic threat to a local white businessman. For Wells, the triple lynching of Calvin McDowell, Tom Moss, and Henry Stewart made plain the masking function of the rape charge in lynching. Wells (and later protesters) would focus relentlessly on the fact that less than 29 percent of all lynchings even involved the charge of rape.

Gender and Sexual Elements

Wells understood lynching as sometimes arbitrary, sometimes tactical terrorism against an entire race of people and a particular assault on black males and black "manhood." In this context, the concept of a "race's manhood" evoked a historically specific set of male social functions (voting, economic independence, and protecting dependents) and symbolized the prestige of an entire community. On a practical level, lynching usually targeted individual black men. On a symbolic level, the lynching story lied about the source of sexual and violent aggression in the South. "This cry [of rape] has had its effect," noted Wells bitterly in *Southern Horrors*. "It has closed the heart, stifled the conscience, warped the judgement and hushed the voice of press and pulpit on the subject of lynch law throughout this 'land of liberty.'" Wells showed that mobs aimed especially at the "subjugation of the young manhood of the race." She insisted that the so-called black beast rapist was in reality the innocent victim of both white male blood lust and, highlighting a previously suppressed element to the story, white female sexual lust.

In an era partial to "black and white" views of social reality, Wells argued that lynching was both about sex and not about sex. She declared that "mob spirit has grown with the increasing intelligence of the AfroAmerican," and from the annual lynching statistics published in the white press, she showed that even according to whites, the rape charge against black men was neither dominant nor adequately proven in lynching cases. Wells also revised the connection between sexual order and social order proposed by the lynching-for-rape story. *Southern Horrors* "reduced to plain English" her belief that white mobs lynched the black man "not because he is always a despoiler of virtue, but because he succumbs to the smiles of white women." Thus the pamphlet provided "a defense for the Afro-American Sampsons who suffer themselves to be betrayed by white Delilahs." It was simply not their fault.

Wells's evidence for consensual sexual liaisons between black men and white women provoked negrophobes' worst nightmare of miscegenation. Through the acknowledgment—even tacit endorsement—of the activities of "white Juliets [and] colored Romeos," she redeployed the white supremacist narrative of race mixing as a story of potential racial equality. Instead of marking the beginning of the end of Anglo-Saxon civilization, Wells reread interracial sex as a signifier of a shared culture and common humanity of all people. At the "bottom of this [lynching] business," argued Wells, was "the fact that coloured men, advancing as they are in intelligence and position, have become attractive to certain classes of white women. . . ."

Frederick Douglass's Position

In *Southern Horrors*, white women appeared as neither passive nor passionless but as agents of racism and illicit sexual desire—not unlike white men. Black women were presented as full historical subjects whose being was violated through assault—much like black men. Muting gender difference, these constructions privileged the racial divide to make the case about unequal power between blacks and whites. Yet at other moments Wells mocked the notion of settled racial distinctions—the supposed "black and white of it"—by pointing to ongoing sexual contact across the color line, to the growing class of mixed-race southerners (herself included), and to cases when white men committed crimes with "their faces blackened." By contesting and refiguring the boundaries between public/private, male/female, black/white, *Southern Horrors* made visible information about sex and power hidden within the conventional lynching story. . . .

Wells's critique thus reclaimed and updated a powerful construction of black female subjectivity as it broke new analytic ground on lynching and southern sexual politics. She redrew the boundaries between private and public on the issues of race and sex and, in so doing, remapped the authority of the black woman intellectual. By insisting that lynching and rape constituted connected domains of racial oppression, Wells rewrote the dominant southern narrative about race relations and female subjectivity in powerfully unsettling terms. Those uncomfortable with a black woman out of (her) place quickly moved to reprimand or silence her. Indeed, the racist Memphians who wrecked her press office also threatened Wells with a lynching replete with castration—"a surgical operation with pair of tailor's shears"—since they assumed that the speaker of such strong words was male.

The Personal Toll on Wells

Like white Memphians, many white Americans ignored Wells's message of black suffering in the South and instead attacked the messenger. White criticism of Wells vividly expressed the racist sexism black women faced in the 1890s. Transgressive white females were viewed as "unsexed"; black females were assumed to be sexually loose. These two images formed ideological counterpoints in rhetorical moves designed to discredit and control unacceptable female speech. White supremacists defined any person who failed to condemn sex across the color line as a dangerous race-mixer. For relating information about illicit interracial sex to white audiences in 1893–94, southern racists labeled Wells a "black harlot" in search of a "white husband," a "strumpet," a "saddle-colored Sapphira [*sic*]," an "adventuress of a decidedly shady character," and "a prostitute bent on miscegenation." The *New York Times* disparaged her as a "slanderous and nasty-minded mulatress." Even northern white women who protested lynching at this time were ridiculed in the South as "the short-haired, strident-voiced sisterhood of Boston," [in the *Chicago Inter-Ocean*, 1899].

In this context of heightened racism and volatile gender politics, few people, white or black, were comfortable with Wells's treatment of sex and race. In her autobiography, Wells recalled that a "delegation" of black men in New York City asked her in 1894 to "put the soft pedal on charges against white women and their relations with black men." Apparently they felt she unduly complicated and sensationalized the already difficult job of ending lynching. Some black women understood Wells's findings about these liaisons as evidence not for liberalized sexual contact across the color line but for better policing of it. "The Afro-American shall be taught, that whatever folly a white woman may commit the suspicion of participation in that folly means torture and death for him," decreed the Ladies' Home Circle of the A.M.E. [African Methodist Episcopal] Church in St. Paul, Minnesota, in 1894.

In general, the black community welcomed Wells's statistical refutation of the rape charge. Yet at a time when hundreds of blacks were being murdered each year in the South, much of the commentary on Wells's work took shape not around the issue of stopping racial violence, which reform-minded readers agreed about, but around gender politics, which were exacerbated by conflict on both sides of the color line. Wells did not hide her femininity (the cover of *Southern Horrors* and [a] letter from [black statesman and author] Frederick Douglass calling her a "Brave woman!" announced it), but neither did she base her authority on essentialist claims about womanhood or female moral superiority over men. . . .

Antilynching Issue Generates Gender Anxiety

Because male power and community prestige (black and white) were at stake in the lynching scenario, African American women's initiative against racial violence promoted gender anxiety. As an intellectual and social project, Wells's antilynching work blurred the boundaries between public and private on issues and responsibilities that were ideally, if not always neatly, coded and divided by gender. Wells's work created anxiety because it destabilized gender dualisms and racial hierarchies and thereby threatened the very terms by which power, order, and legitimacy were understood by many middle-class Americans, black or white, clubwomen or clergy. Wells's exposé of white women's illicit sexual initiatives across the color line caused America's most influential woman, Frances E. Willard (president of the Woman's Christian Temperance Union), to publicly admonish Wells for attacking the ideological pillar of white women's reform: female moral purity. White supremacists lashed out at the specter of an unloosed black female—among the most disempowered of Americans—as a dangerous menace to racial purity and the sexual-social order. And as [the racist laws and attitudes known collectively as] Jim Crow hardened in the early twentieth century, a pattern of gender tension and black female creativity seemed to emerge around the lynching question in African American communities.

For example, in 1915, the *Chicago Defender* lamented the rarity of black men's forcible resistance to mobs, which, according to one writer, required fighting unto death. "Since there are no men, women come to the front; protect the weaklings that still wear the pants from the lynch mobs." When a mob searched out a boy in a black neighborhood for a lynching in Louisiana, the next year, the paper reported that "several girls and women of the Race saw the mob coming and they hid the children till things cooled down. They jeered the mob and refused to run. The men were at the mills working." When human life was at stake, black men and women resisted by whatever means were at hand. But in the aftermath of lynchings and particularly where issues of community prestige and leadership were at stake, gender shaped and defined ideal responses.

Over time, gender anxiety, so easily sparked in the tinderbox context of extreme racism, undermined Ida B. Wells's authority and access to resources within the ranks of American reform.

The Riot Against Chinese Immigrants in Nevada

Sue Fawn Chung and Elmer Rusco

In the late nineteenth and early twentieth centuries, the American West was opening up and becoming more populated. Farmers and miners went to find what they hoped would be better futures. With them came people prepared to make a living providing goods and services. In the early American West, Chinese immigrants played an important, but unappreciated, role in sustaining burgeoning communities. Many of them set up small businesses to provide services that settlers needed, such as laundries. But the Chinese immigrants were often the butt of jokes and the victims of cruelty. The riot in Tonopah, Nevada, in 1903 was just such an incident. A group of white settlers felt threatened by the Chinese families coexisting with them, and they attacked the Chinese one night. Property was damaged, people were hurt and put out of their homes, and one man was killed.

Sue Fawn Chung and Elmer Rusco describe the town and population of Tonopah in the years leading up to the riot. In describing the riot, they also tell about the trial and the outcome for the Chinese in that area after the dust had settled. Chung is an associate professor of history at the University of Nevada–Las Vegas. She has written numerous articles about Chinese American history. Rusco is a professor emeritus at the University of Nevada–Reno. His field of scholarly expertise is civil rights and racism.

On the night of September 15, 1903, several members of the labor union marched into Tonopah's Chinatown and ordered the Chinese residents to leave. Sixty-six-year-old

Sue Fawn Chung and Elmer Rusco, "The Anti-Chinese Riot in Tonopah, Nevada, 1903," *Chinese America: History and Perspectives*, 2003, p. 35ff. Copyright © 2003 Chinese Historical Society of America. Reproduced by permission of the author.

Zhang Bingliang (Chong Bing Long, also called Wing Sing, after the name of his laundry), who had lived in the United States for more than thirty years, was too old to move quickly from his "wash house–residence," so the mob, led by E. M. "Al" Arandall, a rival laundryman and president of Tonopah Labor Union No. 224, robbed him, severely beat him with two pistols and a hatchet, drove him out of town, beat him further, and left him in the desert. Two days later, the deputy constable found his badly bruised body. His skull had been smashed and an artery severed. Although the 1882 Chinese Exclusion Act and its additions had lessened the threat of Chinese labor competition, the impending talks about renewed treaty agreements with China scheduled for 1903–04 revived anti-Chinese sentiments. Anti-Chinese feelings remained strong among some labor union members because of the economic competition, economic downturn, and continued racist beliefs and ideology. This laid the foundation for the 1903 riot. . . .

Social Context of Tonopah

According to census manuscript records of 1910, most of the Chinese in Tonopah were laundrymen or cooks, with a few in scattered occupations, such as boardinghouse owners, house servants, vegetable peddlers, wood packers, restaurant owners, grocers, merchants, and laborers. Chinese cooks and restaurants owners had an advantage over their non-Chinese competition because they often got fresh produce from Chinese growers. The laundries, whose services were crucial to mining communities, did not require a large capital investment, but washing clothes was a demanding, seven-days-a-week occupation. Competition for laundry work arose throughout the West, and Tonopah was no exception. A few laundrymen became prosperous, but most were able to earn only a living wage. Many Chinese laundrymen lived in the back of their shops, as was true for Zhang Bingliang and his assistant Zhang Baiwei (Ah Sam or Bok Wai in the newspapers).

Anti-Chinese sentiment was found among members of the Miners' Union and Labor Union of Tonopah. Raising the banner of the "Yellow Peril," so familiar in the 1870s–90s, the presidents and financial secretaries of both unions jointly endorsed the following declaration, which was published in the January 3, 1903 *Bonanza*:

BE IT KNOWN TO ALL PERSONS:

That the Miners' and Labor Unions of Tonopah, Nevada, view with alarm the inroads that the Chinese labor is making in our fair city, by securing the work that should be done by the willing hands of our own people, especially in laundries, restaurants, hotels, and as household help.

And, whereas, we now have plenty of hotels, restaurants, and a union steam laundry and several white women who are doing laundry business at their home, where Chinese labor is not employed—

We, the undersigned, members of said organizations, by order of our respective unions, do hereby appeal and request all union men and women and the public generally in and around the fair city of Tonopah who are in sympathy with organized labor, to cease their patronage of Chinese restaurants, laundrys, [sic] and all places where Chinese is [sic] employed, thus giving our own race a chance to live.

Anti-Chinese feelings mounted throughout the early months of 1903. These sentiments were heightened by the proposed construction of the Tonopah Railroad, scheduled for completion in 1904, which was expected to use Chinese laborers and to link the mining town to major cities. Nearby Goldfield, founded in 1903, took note of this threat and in 1905 passed a local law prohibiting Asians from disembarking from the train that passed through town. In 1903, most union members favored boycotting businesses that were owned or operated by Chinese or that employed Chinese workers. As in most organizations advocating discrimination, a few felt that peaceful means were not sufficient and favored violence to drive the Chinese out of town.

The Anti-Chinese Riot

On the night of September 15, 1903, a group of thirty to fifty men or more, believed to all be union members, gathered at the lower end of Tonopah and marched into Chinatown, located at the northern end of town. They demanded that the Chinese leave immediately or at least within twenty-four hours. A few hours later, a smaller group entered Chinatown and broke into every Chinese-occupied house, with the exception of the home of Doctor Wo On Hi and the houses of a few Chinese who lived in other parts of the city. The headline of the *Miner* for September 19, 1903 read: "Chinese at the Mercy of a Mob." The headline of the *Bonanza* of the same date read "Gang of Thugs Attack Chinese Quarter." The leaders of the town were appalled at the action, and the newspapers reflected this sentiment in the headlines.

The newspapers gave detailed coverage to the riot, the discovery of Zhang Bingliang's body, the seventeen-day preliminary hearing in Tonopah, and the grand jury trial in Belmont's County Courthouse. Other newspapers in Nevada also carried the story, thus focusing public attention on the incident. The *Miner* was more conservative and often more thorough in its coverage of the trial. The story started out as front-page news. The *Bonanza* was much more sensational in its coverage, and on September 19, 1903, when the story was first published, the editor highlighted James L. Butler's telegram from San Francisco: "If what I read be true regarding abuses of Chinese, it is an outrage to the people of Tonopah. If the people do not fight this case I hope they may never prosper. I will give $500 to any fund for prosecution of the mob, and an additional

$500 in case of conviction." When the founder of the town took this stand, others joined him and the community became divided over the issue of the guilt of the arrested men.

In the same spirit, a mass meeting of concerned citizens was held on September 16 and the following statement was adopted:

WHEREAS, at a meeting of the citizens of Tonopah, Nevada, held pursuant to the call on Wednesday, September 16, 1903, a committee was authorized and appointed to adopt resolutions denouncing the action of the mob, which raided the Chinese quarters of Tonopah on the night of September 15, 1903, murdered an inoffensive Chinaman, beat, mutilated and terrorized a number of others, and robbed and otherwise maltreated them.

Therefore, we, the committee so appointed, hereby present the following resolutions as expressive of sentiment of the people of Tonopah in denunciation of said mob and its atrocious work.

RESOLVED, That the citizens of Tonopah view with horror and denounce in unmeasured terms the outrageous and brutal acts (which according to all the present evidence) have been committed.

That the citizens of Tonopah regard this act as not alone an atrocious violation of the law, but also a heinous crime against inoffensive people, against humanity and civilization.

That the people of Tonopah will support the officers of the law in all possible ways in their efforts to bring the criminals to justice.

The resolution brought words of praise from the editor of the *Desert News*:

The citizens of Tonopab, Nev., [sic] have done well in protesting in mass meeting against the outrages of the mob, that drove the Chinamen out of town, plundering their residences, and, as it seems, murdered one of their number. When such acts of violence are reported from China against "foreign devils" [white men], they arouse indignation and demand revenge. They ought to be doubly avenged when professed "Christians" are the perpetrators of the outrages. We hope the officers of Tonopah will not rest until justice is done in full measure.

The Miners' Union and Labor Union leaders quickly denied that the unions were connected with the outrage, despite the fact that most of the seventeen men arrested were union members and two—E. M. Arandall, president of the Tonopah Labor Union No. 224, and Frank Billings, the Labor Union's recording secretary—were officers. . . .

Zhang Bingliang's Death

The main focus of the news was the death of the sixty-six-year-old laundryman Zhang Bingliang. He had operated the Wing Sing Laundry just behind the Miners' Union Hall and had lived with Charlie Chung and Zhang Baiwei, his assistant in the laundry. Zhang Bingliang, also known as Wing Sing (the name of his laundry), was interested in mining and had purchased Lots 13 and 14, Block G, an undivided 1/2 interest in the "D.D.," an undivided 1/6 interest in the Veteran Lode, and an undivided 1/3 interest in the Stypathia from Charlie Chung. He later sold the two lots to Key Pittman, one of Tonopah's leading citizens and a prosecuting attorney who assisted in the preliminary hearing.

On that fateful night, two men entered Zhang Bingliang's home and severely beat the Chinese laundryman and his assistant. The two assailants, along with four to six others, drove the two Chinese men about a mile out into the desert and beat them some more. Bleeding and disoriented, Zhang Bingliang wandered northward in the direction of Sodaville; after 3 miles of walking, his trail marked by blood, he died in a wash not far from the main road. Two days later, Constable Scott Hickey found his body. Many of the citizens of Tonopah were angry, but others sided with the rioters.

On September 26, the preliminary hearing began for the seventeen arrested men: E. M. Arandall, H. Zumstein, William Lang, C. Gallagher, Charles White, John Millick, A. E. Fetter, O. M. Jackson, John Hill, Frank Weiss, A. M. Bradshaw, Omar Sinks, C. M. Maxwell, I. C. Cushman, H. A. Breusing, F M. Billings, and A. Wilson, the only African-American involved in the case. Arandall, Millick, and Wilson were charged with murder; the others were charged with rioting and assault. The names are significant because they represent a cross section of the ethnic groups that made up the population of Tonopah. . . .

Outcome of the Trial

In the end, only six men—E. M. Arandall, a laundry owner; E. R. Shellingberger, a bookkeeper; W A. Lang; A. Wilson, an Afro-American cook; A. M. Bradshaw; and O. M. Jackson, a restaurant worker—were charged with assault and murder. The case of the *State v. Arandall et al.* was tried before the grand jury for five days in Belmont, the county seat, in December 1903. District Attorney C. L. Richards and Associate Counsel P. M. Bowler, Jr., represented the State of Nevada; C. F. Reynolds and S. E. Vermilyea represented the six defendants. Vermilyea was allowed to talk for a considerable time on the issue of labor and the Chinese question at the trial, despite the fact that it was not relevant to a murder case. This indicated how powerful these concerns and racism were at the time. Despite the eyewitness accounts of Zhang Baiwei and the other witnesses, a verdict of "Not Guilty" for each of the six men was returned by the jury after one hour and fifteen minutes. Although the *Miner* simply stated the results, the *Bonanza* pointed out that the crowded courtroom was filled with "the wildest enthusiasm" when the verdict was read. . . .

There were other cases that were not covered in the newspapers as well. Two men, Xie Liansheng and Tan Liansheng, not only lost property and cash but incurred medical expenses and loss of potential income. For Xie Liansheng, who incurred $400 in medical expenses resulting from a severe beating, these medical expenses represented approximately seven months of income. Fellow laundryman Tan Liansheng incurred the most medical expenses—$550—the result of being beaten by four men with guns. Charley Hey, a grocer who not only lost cash ($230) and valuables (gold watch $75, gold chain $15, pistol $15) but also suffered serious business losses (estimated at $1,800), for a total of $2,135, suffered the largest known losses. Cheong Long Restaurant owners Yee Kwai (also known as Joe Quin) and Loni Kim (also known as Young Louie) reported a combined loss of $2,580, which included destruction of furniture and utensils ($700), business loss ($1,500), rent liability ($100 per month), goods destroyed ($260), and cash stolen ($20). Three partners in a restaurant business in Gold Mountain, some 6 miles from Tonopah, also suffered losses totaling $800. These reports indicate that the mob violence and loss of property were more serious than what was reported in the local newspapers.

Yee Tom Shee, a married woman, never had her story reported in the newspapers. She claimed a loss of $399 worth of items, mostly jewelry, including a diamond ring, gold watch, gold earrings, and gold bracelets. One wonders if the public would have been more outraged if they had known that the rioters had accosted a woman. . . .

Tonopah Riot Inspired Others

The success of the rioters in their "Not Guilty" verdict inspired others to try the same course of action. On December 18, 1904, another group of Euro-Americans ordered the Chinese and Japanese residents of Goldfield, Nevada, to leave and prohibited the Asian workers on the Carson and Colorado railroad from entering town, justifying their actions by saying that "miners the world over refuse to place themselves in competition with cheap unskilled labor and for this just reason it is thought the order to move on was given." Again the Chinese consul general in San Francisco and the Chinese minister appealed to the secretary of state to call this to the attention of the authorities in Nevada, but the result was the continuation of a strong anti-Asian sentiment in Goldfield. Years later, when Billy Ford [a victim of the Tonopah riot] went to Goldfield with his children, Jim and Bessie, their lasting memory was of the anti-Chinese atmosphere that prevailed there. For Bessie, it was a comfort to return home to the friendly environment of Tonopah.

Tonopah After the Riot

Although the violence in Tonopah was one of many examples of injustice from the Chinese perspective, the Tonopah community was more cordial to some of the Chinese in town after the riot. Tonopah's population grew rapidly with the advent of the railroad, and an estimated 10,000 people lived there in 1905–07. A series of fires and the Panic of 1907, when two of the three Tonopah banks closed, marked the beginning of the town's decline, and by 1910 the population had dwindled to 3,900. The 1910 census manuscript showed a total of 53 Chinese living in Tonopah: 44 Chinese adult males (27 of whom were married, in addition to 2 widowers), including 3 sons of Billy Ford (Tim, James, and George Washington); and 11 females, including 2 married adult females, 3 daughters of Billy Ford (Bessie, Rose, and Lillian), and 1 half-Chinese, half-Shoshone female teenager. However, even in 1913, there were two Chinese merchandising firms, Foo Yuen and Co. and Fook Lee and Co., still thriving in Tonopah. Many of the Chinese involved in the hearing and trial stayed in Tonopah for several years, and a few, like Billy Ford and Charlie Chung, remained there until their deaths and were buried there. In contrast, the

1910 census manuscript does not list any of the arrested riot-ers, who probably left town shortly after the trial or because of the 1907 Panic.

The riot actually had some benefits for some. Billy Ford, for example, gained community recognition. The births of his next four children were announced in the local press. His children grew up in a relatively tolerant atmosphere and had many, often lifelong, friends. They made friends with the other children in school. "My sisters chummed with the Ford girls," wrote Norman Douglass Money, "while I played marbles, spun tops and broke burros with the boys. Tim [Ford] . . . and I were pupils together in Professor Carol's violin class. . . . I did well enough to play third violin, . . . the professor play[ed] first and Tim . . . play[ed] an excellent second." Another classmate of the Fords recalled, "We were all children of immigrants from different countries so we were all alike." Mrs. Billy Ford was told that if anyone ever gave her any problems, she should see the sheriff immediately, and a close relationship developed between the Ford family and the sheriff's family. When Billy died, the headline of his April 14, 1922 obituary, published in the *Bonanza*, read: "[A] Real Pioneer [of] Southern Nevada, [Who] Was Honored and Respected Among Associates, RAISED A SPLENDID FAMILY, Was Universally Liked and [Whose] Demise is Regretted by the Pioneers of the State." This was an impressive tribute to a member of a minority group that had been targeted for removal from the town.

The 1903 anti-Chinese riot in Tonopah did not give the injured Chinese residents any legal remedies, but it did highlight the discriminatory court procedures and reckless actions of the Labor and Miners' Unions. The Chinese found some help from their official representatives, but banded together in mutual support just as they had elsewhere in the American West. As in all legal cases of the period, the expenses for litigation were beyond their combined means. Some of the Euro-

American leaders of Tonopah went out of their way to create a friendlier atmosphere for their Chinese residents, and Billy Ford's experience was probably typical of how something good can come from something bad.

The Town of Jasper, Texas, After James Byrd's Murder

David Grann

In the summer of 1998, a black man named James Byrd was dragged to his death behind a truck by three white supremacists. The incident met with a nationwide outcry about hate crime, prejudice, and race relations in a so-called modern age. The crime took place in the small Texas town of Jasper, which soon found itself in the middle of a media frenzy. It also became a symbolic battleground where the Ku Klux Klan, the New Black Panthers, and the Black Muslims met face-to-face. Journalist David Grann headed to Jasper in the days leading up to the rally where the three groups would meet. He talked to local Klansmen and the Black Muslim leader. In an article for the New Republic, *Grann related his experiences and his reflections on the town of Jasper in the wake of Byrd's murder. Grann's articles have appeared in such publications as the* New Republic, *the* New York Times Magazine, *and the* New Yorker.

Darrell Flinn wouldn't say it was an omen, exactly. But the fires did start right around the time those three white boys allegedly tied that Negro behind a pickup truck and dragged him for three miles down Huff Creek Road in nearby Jasper, Texas. They burned all night, sometimes for more than a week. Helicopters swept down, spraying water, though it didn't seem to do much good. It hadn't rained hard for more than two months, and all it took was a bolt of lightning, the flick of a cigarette, or a spark from an engine before another blaze broke out.

On this Tuesday, a teenager had lit a fire right there in Vidor, where Flinn lived, sending up flames from the yellow pine trees even as he sat out with his three little kids at Smith Lake to cool off in the sweltering heat. "It's so hot we can't even burn a cross," Flinn said, glancing at me. "There's a state ordinance against any loose fires."

Klansmen Plan Rally

That, of course, meant no cross-burning at this Saturday's rally, though it didn't much matter to Flinn. Everyone in the media would be there anyway. He'd already been on MSNBC, CNBC, CBS, *Hard Copy*. Even a reporter from Italy had called that morning. "How do you say nigger in Italian, 'negre'?" he mused aloud.

I didn't say anything, and watched as he took off his combat boots and T-shirt and exposed his belly to the sun. "What do you think's gonna happen in Jasper?" he asked. "You think those niggers with shotguns will show up?"

Looking up from my notebook, I shrugged and asked how many from his Klan would show up.

Flinn said he didn't like to make predictions because if he said forty, and only twenty showed up, it would seem like the event was a failure. "I estimate a hundred and forty," he said, suddenly throwing away his caution. He started to tick off the other groups, pausing after each for emphasis: Alabama White Knights . . . Missouri's New Order Knights . . . America's Invisible Empire . . . The American Knights . . . North Georgia White Knights. . . .

I got to Texas two weeks after James Byrd Jr. was dragged to his death for no other apparent reason than he was black, and after Jesse Jackson and the Rev. Al Sharpton and NAACP President Kweisi Mfume and California Congresswoman Maxine Waters and Transportation Secretary Rodney Slater had come to pay their respects, and after the president of the United States had sent his condolences, and after Dennis Rodman had offered to pay for Byrd's funeral, and after Don King had donated $100,000 to a memorial fund, and after the KKK had announced it would rally in Jasper to raise white people's pride, and after the New Black Panther Party and the Black Muslims had vowed to show up with shotguns to arm the black people of Jasper against the Klan.

I wasn't sure exactly why I was there, other than that everyone else from the media was there—convinced, perhaps, that the Old South was rising again, at least for an afternoon. Before I got to Jasper, though, I had stopped in Vidor, about an hour away, because that was where the old Klan still purportedly thrived and where Darrell Flinn, the imperial wizard of the Knights of the White Kamellia, had moved recently with his wife and three boys. . . .

Black Panthers and Black Muslims Prepare to Fight Back

When I arrived at the SHAPE Community Center in southeast Houston the next night, a half-dozen Black Panthers and Muslims were already loading their weapons—shotguns and street sweepers and AR-15s—as they plotted strategy for Saturday's showdown in the town square. "The white man will confront something new in Jasper," proclaimed Quanell X, a twenty-seven-year-old former youth minister of the Nation of Islam and the current leader of the militant Black Muslims. "Well-trained, well-organized, and disciplined black men."

As Quanell stood, two guards clad in army fatigues toting twelve-gauge shotguns rushed to his side. Unlike his troops, the general carried none of the paraphernalia of war. He wore an Armani suit and a diamond-studded gold watch.

As he filed past me, one of the guards said, "Search the cracker before he gets in the car." I pulled my pad and pen out of my pocket and spread my arms.

Outside, we climbed into an onyx-colored Mercedes and headed for the Fox television studio, where Quanell would debate on-air the infamous Klansman, Michael Lowe. While we sped along the back streets of Houston, looking through the tinted windows at the black kids sitting on their porches smoking cigarettes in the 100-degree heat, I asked Quanell X why he felt compelled to go to Jasper if most people there didn't want him. "It's simple," he said. "We want to say to the KKK that your days of intimidating, harassing, and instigating violence against black people is all over. . . . We are willing and ready—*take this left here*—to fight the Klan by any means necessary. . . . That if you want a war—*here! here!*—we'll be damned if we won't give you one."

"What about the black pastors from Jasper who don't want you to come?" I asked.

"I don't give two cents about what some weak-kneed, handkerchief-head, Negro pastor thinks of me. I'm only interested in what God thinks of me."

If the Ku Klux Klan had learned that the best way to get attention was to advocate hatred camouflaged by kindness, then the Black Panthers and Muslims had learned that the best way to get attention was to advocate peace through violence. At the television studio, where Quanell X had become a regular in the days after Byrd's killing, the militant leader disappeared into the bathroom and reemerged wearing a white bow tie.

While a technician connected his earpiece, Quanell and the rest of us could hear Lowe's trademark lisp, testing his mike from another studio in Texas. Then came another voice, the host's, even louder: "The KKK and a so-called group of black radicals are heading to a town where a black man was allegedly killed by white supremacists. Will there be more bloodshed? . . . Up next!" Quanell narrowed his eyes at the camera's white light. "Okay," said a producer in the control room. "Hold onto your shirts—and thank God they can't touch each other."

Klan Leadership Prepares to Meet Opposition

The next morning another fire broke out, this one right near Jasper. "It's supposed to get even hotter," said Flinn. I'd stopped by one last time for breakfast with the imperial wizard at Gary's Coffee Shop. There, Flinn introduced me to James, the current grand dragon of the Knights of the White Kamellia, who would only give me his first name. Unlike Flinn, James didn't look much like the new "improved" Klan: His hair and eyes were a muted yellow, his teeth brown and crooked, and tattoos were stenciled all along his arms. When I asked him if he'd bring a shotgun to the rally, he lit his second Marlboro of the morning and said, "I'll probably bring something just in case." Each time the talk took such a turn, Flinn nudged him with his elbow. Later, when I got up to leave, James looked suspiciously at my scribbled handwriting and asked, "What religion are you, anyway?" I didn't say anything. "You gotta be somethin'," he said, leaning across the table. I glanced at Flinn, then back at James, whose veins were tightening in his arms. I thought for a moment of my bar mitzvah. "Episcopalian," I said. . . .

[The morning of the rally] something strange was happening in Jasper: While the hotels filled with visitors, most of the locals were fleeing town. Unlike the late 1950s and 1960s, when people rose up from within the very fabric of Southern society—blacks from the streets and the churches, the Klan from the local businesses and bars—Jasper's race war was being fueled entirely by outsiders, by a handful of atomized groups. On this Saturday morning, the journalists came in droves, from Paris and Tokyo and Bonn and New York and New Orleans. By 10:00 A.M., they vastly outnumbered the spectators and law enforcement officers and swarmed from one side of the square to the other, searching for angry white men or black men or any men to film. "This is a joke," said a journalist holding a mike. "Where's all the f--kin' bloodshed?"

When a lone Klansman finally arrived with a young boy, carrying Confederate flags, an army of reporters surrounded him. "That's it," prodded one cameraman, "show us the tattoo.... Can you give us a side shot? ... Perfect.... Perfect." But, as the press pushed closer, the Klansman's teenage companion began to tremble. "Do you hate me?" shouted a black reporter. "No," the boy said sheepishly. "Then who do you hate?" He looked around at the cameras, searching for his friend. On the verge of tears, he blurted out, "Everybody." ...

Clash in Jasper

After an hour of this, the press moved on, bored and listless. As I considered leaving, twenty-five Klansmen, led by Flinn, appeared in black and white robes, surrounded by a phalanx of police wearing riot gear. Then came the Panthers, toting rifles and chanting, "Black power." "We can take these bastards!" screamed one. "We can run over the damn police and take their asses!" There were no more than a handful of them, but, upon spotting the cameras, they began to charge—unleashing a stampede of more than 300 reporters. I chased after Quanell X in his ochre Armani suit and matching alligator shoes, shouting questions he couldn't hear. I climbed onto a bench for a better view. From there, I could see a Panther being filmed by a Klansman who was being filmed by the police—all of whom were being filmed by the media.

After a momentary retreat, the seven Panthers charged again. And again, I was running, pushing against the barricades to keep up with them. I saw a girl fall and a cameraman step on her.

Shaken, I made my way across the square, away from the crowd, which was still racing from side to side in a kind of unrehearsed theater. I found my car and drove through town, out into the country, past the local paper and the sheriff's station, until I stopped outside a small wooden house, where the

Byrds lived. Two police guards stood outside. "How are things in town?" one guard asked, looking at my sweat-stained clothes.

"Not so good," I said, though the more I thought about it, the more I realized how little the chaos in the square had anything to do with the killing of James Byrd, or with anything real.

The Crime Scene

I asked for directions out to Huff Creek Road—an unmarked street on the outskirts of town. I crossed over a bridge straddling a trough of dust and passed several run-down houses, a Baptist church, and a cemetery. Finally, below a row of yellow pine trees, I pulled over and began to walk back toward town, past where they had allegedly beaten Byrd and tied his ankles to a chain. After a half-mile or so, I came upon an orange painted circle, then another, and another, marking where the police had found Byrd's severed head and torso and limbs. There was still blood encrusted in the dirt. The crime scene ran for two-and-a-half miles, and, as I neared the end, I felt the first drops of rain.

The Disabled as a Target of Hate

Kathi Wolfe

Most hate crimes target victims the attackers see as weak, physically or socially. Because the disabled appear to be powerless to defend themselves, they are targeted for verbal and physical attacks. The hatred toward this group of people comes from the attacker's belief that the disabled person is less than a person and unworthy of living a normal life. Their hostility comes from a perception of weakness and helplessness in the victim, added to the fact that someone with a physical or mental disability is less likely to be able to defend himself. Journalist and poet Kathi Wolfe discusses the mind-set of such attackers and what can be done to protect the disabled against hate crimes. As a blind woman and a lesbian, Wolfe knows firsthand what it is like to be the target of hate and discrimination. She has written numerous articles on subjects related to challenges experienced by the disabled.

"Move, blind lady," a man hissed at me as he twisted my arm and grabbed my cane. He threw my cane down the escalator, which was taking me to the subway in Washington, D.C. He spat on me and growled, "You people belong in concentration camps."

I knew that some people dislike those of us with disabilities, but before this encounter at the subway, I had no idea that this hostility could take the form of such rabid hatred. I had heard about neo-Nazi skinheads from news reports, usually from some place in Europe. But as I wiped the spit from my arm and groped for my cane, I saw what I hadn't seen be-

Kathi Wolfe, "Bashing the Disabled: The New Hate Crime," *The Progressive*, vol. 59, No. 11, November 1995, pp. 292–317. Copyright © 1995 by The Progressive, Inc. Reproduced by permission of The Progressive, 409 East Main Street, Madison, WI 53703, www.progressive.org.

fore: hate crimes can happen here—in a respectable, middle-class neighborhood in the United States.

If my story were unique, it could be shrugged off as an isolated incident of disability-bashing. But disability advocates across the country say this isn't the case.

Prejudicial Backlash Against Disabled and Others

"Today in America, there's a frightening backlash against not only disabled people, but minorities, women, gays, and all those whose civil rights need protection," asserts Justin Dart Jr., a former chairman of the President's Committee on Employment of People with Disabilities.

A column by Paul Hollander that appeared in the *Wall Street Journal* entitled, "We Are All (Sniffle, Sniffle) Victims Now," conveys the spirit of this backlash. Hollander writes, "If we add them all up—women, blacks, Hispanics, Native Americans, the disabled, homosexuals, AIDS victims, the homeless, the children of abusive parents, the overweight, etc.—it would emerge that not more than 15 percent of the population of the U.S. is free of the injuries of victimhood."

What's fueling the backlash against the disabled? Resentment of the Americans with Disabilities Act (ADA), signed by President George [H.W.] Bush in 1990, say disability-community leaders.

"We shouldn't be surprised by the backlash," says Marca Bristo, chair of the National Council on Disability. "It happens in our society whenever a constituency fights for its civil rights. The ADA gave us our rights; we can't be turned away from jobs or public accommodations because of our disability. So now we're feeling the effects of this not-unexpected backlash."

Hate Crimes Against Disabled on the Rise

One manifestation of this backlash is hate crimes against the disabled, says Dart, who has polio. "We've become a scapegoat," he says. "Some people who don't wish to hear about our country's economic or social problems—who want to ignore civil-rights issues—blame disabled people for these problems. Sometimes that gets acted out in hateful rhetoric or hate crimes." . . .

Hostility against the disabled is increasingly common even in public, says Jean Parker, executive director of the Colorado Cross-Disability Coalition.

Parker, who is blind, knows this firsthand. One day, she was standing with her guide dog at a bus stop in Denver. As they were waiting for the bus, she says, "Someone silently approached and deliberately kicked my guide dog in the kidneys. I have no vision; because the person who hurt my dog didn't speak, I couldn't tell if the attacker was a man or woman.

"This was a hate crime. The perpetrator didn't assault or rob me. It was clear that my dog was a guide dog used to assist someone who is blind. This crime was motivated by hatred of blindness and of disability. A man was present who saw my dog being kicked. I tried to get him to give the police a description of the perpetrator, but he declined; he was afraid of retribution."

This fear is one of the reasons why hate crimes are under-reported, says Veronica Robertson, who represents the disability community on the Illinois Hate Crimes Task Force. "People are afraid to tell anybody that they've been the victim of a hate crime because they're scared that the perpetrator will go after them again."

Robertson, a staff member of the Chicago-based advocacy group Access on Living, tells how a hate crime has devastated the life of one disabled person. "He's a quadriplegic in his mid-thirties who lives in subsidized housing on the north side of Chicago. Every time he goes outside, the same guy beats him up. While he's beating him, he says, 'I don't want you out here, you cripple. I don't like your kind. You people bring down the community.' This man is terrified of leaving his apartment building because he knows he'll be beaten and verbally abused. And he's too frightened to report the hate crime because the perpetrator has told him, 'If you tell anyone about this, I'll beat your ass.'"

Hate crimes against disabled people aren't being committed only in low-income, urban areas, Robertson says. "There's hate crime in the suburbs, too."

She describes one couple's futile effort to live in a Chicago suburb: "They were a husband and wife who both used wheelchairs. They had bought a house and needed to put in a ramp to make it wheelchair-accessible. People in the township came to them and said they didn't want a ramp to be installed because it would interfere with the landscaping. The couple, who weren't violating any zoning rules, said they were going to put the ramp in. Some people in the neighborhood got so angry about this that they threw rocks in the couple's home. They vandalized their house and sent threatening letters to the wife that said, 'Your kind won't last here.' Eventually, the couple gave up trying to live with the harassment and moved away."

FBI to Track Crimes Against Disabled

The Hate Crimes Statistics Act was amended to include bias based on disability, through the legislative efforts of [then] Senate Majority Leader Bob Dole, himself a disabled veteran. The FBI will now collect data about disability-based hate crimes, as well as those based on race, ethnicity, religion, and sexual orientation.

"We'll be helping disability groups understand and identify hate crimes, and we'll be working to make police departments and law-enforcement agencies more knowledgeable about disability and sensitive to disabled people," says James Nolan, the coordinator of hate-crimes training programs for the FBI.

Barbara Faye Waxman, a disability activist who has done extensive research on the issue of hate crimes, says that hate crimes have usually been committed against disabled persons "behind closed doors—in homes and in institutions. Now that people with disabilities are becoming visible—in the workplace, in stores, on the streets—more hate crimes are being committed out in the open."

Resentment Drives Hostility

Waxman, the project director for the National Disability Reproductive Health Access Project in Cupertino, California, places hate crimes against the disabled within the framework of the current backlash. "There's a feeling that disabled people are taking away the rights and resources of those who are more deserving," she says. "Resentment of disabled people is now being publicly expressed—in Congress, the media, in conversation, and in hate crimes."

The idea that people can hate the disabled is hard for many to take seriously, says Lolly Lijewski, of the Metro Center for Independent Living, an advocacy organization for disabled persons in St. Paul, Minnesota. She explains, "We're taught from the time we're kids to pity disabled people—to 'help the handicapped.' So it's difficult to believe that there's hatred out there against people with disabilities," she says. "But some are upset that the disability community is asserting its rights. For example, a businessman recently said in one of our local newspapers that disabled people 'should have three meals a day and a roof over their heads, but I think we have to draw the line somewhere. I don't think that they can have total freedom.' This man isn't advocating the perpetration of hate crimes; but the current climate is fostering the seeds of hatred from which hate crimes grow."

Helen Kutz, director of the client-assistance project of the Office of Handicapped Concerns in Oklahoma City, says, "It's painful for those of us who are disabled to admit that sometimes people hate us. The disability community needs to come to grips with the issue of hate crimes: we may not want to admit it, but hate crimes are happening."

She tells what happened one night to a man she knows with cerebral palsy: "He was walking home after socializing with some of his friends. Suddenly, some guys stopped him, picked him up, threw him in a trash can, and put the lid on it. While they did this, they called out epithets regarding his disability, saying, 'You belong in the trash, you cripple.'

"He got himself out of the trash can, but it took a very long time. The cerebral palsy makes his gait unsteady and affects his speech. Because of his speech defect, he couldn't yell for help."

Targeting the Mentally Disabled

Hostility against those with mental illness and mental retardation is particularly acute. Joseph Rogers, deputy executive director of the Mental Health Association of Southeastern Pennsylvania, says, "This hostility runs the gamut from epithets to fire bombings of group homes for people with mental illness or mental retardation. It comes out of the fear and loathing that people have of those who are different from them. People don't want disabled people living in their communities— especially people with mental illness."

Rogers, a former mental patient, describes an incident that occurred more than twenty years ago when he was living in a group home in Florida. "One night when a friend and I were taking a walk, some guys drove by and threw a Coke bottle at us," he recalls. "The bottle hit my friend, but what hurt more than that was the things that those guys were shouting at us. They were yelling, 'You f--king crazies! Get the f--k out of our neighborhood.'"

Unfortunately, Rogers says, things haven't changed. "Across the country, group homes for mentally ill people are the recipients of threatening phone calls and letters as well as bombs."

For example, in Newark, New Jersey, a notice was taped to the door of a group home which had not yet opened that said, "If you open this home in this neighborhood, we're going to burn this place down." Later a lit firebomb was thrown onto the porch of the home, Rogers says.

Role of Local Politics

During the 1994 elections, campaign literature centering on housing where a number of mentally retarded people lived was distributed in Elizabeth, New Jersey, that preyed upon "public fears and misconceptions about disabled people," says Marshall Bord, assistant executive director of Community Access Unlimited, an advocacy group for people with disabilities based in Elizabeth. "A candidate running for city council put out a flyer that referred to the disabled people living in our housing as 'deranged or demented.' We were incensed that such derogatory, demeaning terms would appear on campaign literature." The candidate who distributed the flyer didn't win the election. But Bord, who is a member of the Elizabeth Human Rights Commission, didn't want matters to stop there. Nor did the other members of the Commission.

Helene Scheuer, executive director of Elizabeth's Human Rights Commission, says that the Commission has asked all candidates in the fall elections whose constituencies include Elizabeth to sign a pledge stating, "I . . . promise not to negatively use race, religion, gender, national origin, sexual preference, or handicapping conditions as an issue in my campaign."

Bord says, "Of course the candidates can't be forced to sign the pledge. But we hope the pledge sends a message that bigotry and hateful literature won't be acceptable in our elections."

While it is well organized on other concerns, the disability community hasn't yet organized around the issue of hate crimes, says Reva Trevino of the Los Angeles County Commission on Human Relations. Trevino works for the Commission's Network Against Hate Crime.

"If a constituency wants to combat hate crime, it must teach its members how to identify and report hate crimes," she says.

Disabled people need to organize, just as gays and lesbians and other targets of violent backlash have organized, to combat hate and to insist on our right to live in a civil society.

Antigay Violence
Is a Cultural Problem

Ritch C. Savin-William

As the public becomes more aware of violence against gays and lesbians, many have questioned why such violence continues. Are these incidents isolated, and what do they say about Americans as a whole? Proponents of educating the public on the issue maintain that knowing more about homosexuals and their experiences will reduce fear and anxiety about them and thus also reduce hate and violence toward them.

In the following article, author and professor Ritch C. Savin-William appeals to his fellow educational professionals to make homosexual awareness and understanding a higher priority. He urges educators to be intentional in the way they teach about—or even speak about—sexuality in the class and in academic works. Savin-William is a professor in and chair of the Department of Human Development at Cornell University.

Sixty-eight percent of North Americans believe the attack against college freshman Matthew Shepard could have happened in their community (Time/CNN Poll, 1998). Within a week of the Wyoming murder, a Colorado State University fraternity mocked Matthew's death in their homecoming parade float by hanging a beaten scarecrow from a fence with a sign, "I am Gay." A lesbian student at St. Cloud State University in Minnesota suffered cuts and bruises after two men attacked her, just hours after an antihate-crimes campus vigil honoring Matthew Shepard. Leonard "Lynn" Vines, a gay drag queen, was shot six times by a group of Baltimore youths who shouted that they did not allow "no drag queen faggot bitches"

Ritch C. Savin-William, "'Matthew Shepard's Death: A Professional Awakening," *Applied Developmental Science*, vol. 3, 1999, pp. 150–54. Copyright © 1999 Lawrence Erlbaum Associates, Inc. Reproduced with permission of Taylor & Francis Books Ltd., conveyed through Copyright Clearance Center, Inc.

in their neighborhood. Leonard survive, but many do not. Liz Seaton, executive director of the Free State Justice Campaign, said in a [1998] press release:

> What happened in Wyoming is happening everywhere and it is happening here. It is time for people to wake up, to recognize that bias does lead to violence, and to take action. Fair-minded citizens must take a stand that anti-gay bias is not acceptable under any circumstances.

Silence Enables Acts of Hate

Could Matthew's murder and the violence against Leonard, the Minnesota lesbian, and many other lesbian, gay, bisexual, and transgender individuals have been prevented? Perhaps. This violence has its roots in our culture's tolerance of children calling each other "faggot" and "dyke," of teachers who do not correct or stop gay-related name calling, and of parents who do not admonish children who have destructive stereotypes and myths about gay people. One need not be a perpetrator of violence to be a murderer. The bystander plays an important role in facilitating expressions of hatred and violence. Several years before Matthew's murder by two Laramie, WY, young adult men, a local billboard advertising guns had been altered from "Shoot a day or two" to "Shoot a gay or two." For over a month, hundreds if not thousands of residents had remained silent, until a visiting gay activist had it erased. How many well-educated, liberal, scholarly men and women had passed the billboard and chose to do nothing? Perhaps a few social scientists were among those who decided to ignore the "humor."

In our silence, we contribute to the figurative and, at times, literal deaths of sexual-minority family members, friends, clients, and colleagues. We perpetuate myths and hatred, if not directly, then by assuming the role of passive bystander. . . .

Sensitivity in the Classroom

Although I appreciate colleagues' efforts to be inclusive when they ask me to give "the gay lecture" in their courses, my strong preference would be for my colleagues to give the lecture themselves. This would indicate to me a deeper level of personal and professional investment and commitment to sexual-minority concerns. Even more appealing than having a "special" lecture or a reading on relevant sexual-minority issues is for teachers to integrate the lives of sexual-minority individuals throughout a course. For example, the topic of adolescent homosexuality is usually confined to a late chapter in adolescent textbooks, under headings titled *Sexuality, Sexual Self, and Sex and Dating*—as if being lesbian, bisexual, gay, or transgender is only about sex. If sexual minorities differ in physical growth characteristics, such as their physical shape and size, then these facts should be discussed in the *"Physical Growth"* chapter. If gay and lesbian adolescents disproportionately face particular difficulties in schools, are harassed by peers, or abuse substances, then these should be discussed in appropriate chapters. If sexual-minority youths have special intellectual or creative abilities and have made significant contributions to our culture, these too should be included. If two adolescents of the same sex fall in love, then the possibility ought to be acknowledged—and a photograph portraying their love should be included as well.

As with many adolescents, sex is important to these youths, but they are more than their sexual preferences, identities, and orientation. The aspect of Matthew that carried the most import to his murderers was his sexual orientation. Matthew, the Minnesota lesbian, and the drag queen are similar to all other adolescents, but at the same time different, because of their sexuality. For example, all youths growing up in North America are aware that the worst putdown is to be called "dyke" or "faggot," and that many parents want their child to be anything but gay. A child with same-sex attractions living under these conditions has to be affected. It affects relations with family, peers, and, perhaps most importantly, the self. In our classrooms and scholarship, we must recognize that sexual-minority individuals are unique as a group, perhaps for biological (brain organization) and environmental (growing up in a homonegative culture) reasons, but also that they differ among themselves in their life trajectories and countless other ways. Whether the course or text is on adolescence or on relationships, infancy, cognition, public policy, or psychopathology, sexual minorities and their lives should neither be ignored nor confined to a singular lecture or reading but integrated within the spectrum of scholarly work. It is the representation of this wholeness that demonstrates the humanity of nonheterosexuals.

Sensitivity in the Professional World

Complacency and sins of omission are omnipresent. Another example from my professional life is illustrative. The Society for Research on Adolescence (SRA) has never invited a speaker to their national conference to discuss any scholarly aspect of growing up gay or lesbian in today's world, and their widely distributed *Journal of Research on Adolescence* has not devoted a special issue to research on sexual-minority youths. In a correspondence with a highly placed officer of SRA about my forthcoming *SRA Newsletter* article in which I advocate that the organization take a proactive stance and include conversations about sexual-minority youths, the officer argued, "SRA is not an advocacy organization, nor, in my opinion, should it be. . . . Although advocating on issues we care deeply about may enhance our moral credibility, more often than not it diminishes our scientific credibility." I disagree—SRA and many other professional organizations are advocates, if even for the status quo; thus, SRA's silence regarding sexual-minority issues is a moral posture. I believe it is within the purview of science and its professional organizations to single out areas, perhaps for moral or ethical considerations, for research attention. Consequently, research on ethnic-racial minorities and women has escalated, in large part because scientific organizations assumed a stance that this needed to be done. I argue that increasing our knowledge about sexual-minority individuals and their communities is one of those worthy areas.

It is my strong belief that it is unconscionable to delay addressing critical scientific concerns of sexual-minority populations simply because no one has volunteered to submit research articles or to give keynote addresses at professional conferences. Rather, those in positions of power must take a *proactive* stance and invite speakers and writers to submit their work. . . . The "highly placed" SRA officer has recommended that I continue to "push" the SRA and the *Journal of Research on Adolescence* to be more inclusive. I only wish that it were not always necessary for members of oppressed groups (including women, racial-ethnic, and religious groups) to ensure that their representation is accurately and fairly presented to those in the majority.

Speak Up When Faced with Exclusion or Hate

When you witness heterocentric or homonegative language or actions, do not turn away. They occur at all levels of discourse, from interpersonal relationships to institutional policies and structures. If your institution does not have an antidiscrimination policy, a resource office or center, faculty or staff groups, courses, library materials, or visibility for sexual-minority populations, choose to change the status quo. Efforts can include active lobbying, organizing, and networking with highly placed officials who share your views. Class announcements about upcoming lectures, meetings, and social events that are of concern to sexual minorities can be very effective in communicating your openness. So, too, nonheterocentric, inclusive language conveys an acceptance of sexual diversity and allows nonheterosexual individuals to feel less alienated. Statements on course syllabi or at the beginning of courses about your nontolerant stance toward antigay acts and your inclusive attitude will help end the silence that was partially responsible for Matthew's death.

In an ideal world, all of us would challenge in whatever ways possible the presumption that sexual minorities are invisible, worthy of denigration, and that "heterosexual allies" do not exist or will not speak up. Failure to do so is to become a bystander—the silent perpetrator who passes, without acting, the billboard that advocates killing gay people.

CHAPTER 2

Hate Groups and Anti-Hate Groups

Chapter Preface

At the age of fourteen, T. J. Leyden joined a skinhead group. He learned to be hateful, menacing, and cruel. He and his fellow skinheads did not hesitate to beat someone brutally merely for giving them a look they did not like. Later, he joined the marines to receive combat and weapons training. Over the course of his years as a skinhead, Leyden had white power tattoos all over his body. He set out to make himself a well-equipped, trained, intimidating hate machine—and he succeeded.

Leyden was not only an active and violent member of his faction, but he was also a recruiter sent to scout out vulnerable, impressionable young men in southern Utah and California. In his speeches, he explained how he broke new recruits by humiliating them and physically assaulting them. Once they were sufficiently belittled, Leyden indoctrinated them as he built them back up with "white power."

One day, when Leyden's toddler son used a racial epithet while watching a children's show, Leyden took note. He began to see the lies of his ideology for what they were. After fifteen years as a neo-Nazi skinhead, Leyden abandoned the group with full knowledge that all of their hatred would be unleashed on him as a traitor of the highest order. When he could not convince his wife to defect with him, he fled to California to be with family members. But a few weeks later, he returned to take his sons because he could not stomach the thought of his boys being groomed to be white supremacists. Since abandoning his faction, he has received numerous death threats, and white supremacists are encouraged to kill him on the spot.

Leyden's determination to turn the tide of his own life grew into a drive to turn the tide of hate groups. Consequently, he has become a speaker on the subject of hate groups, educating and warning teachers, parents, and students. He has even partnered with such organizations as the Museum for Tolerance and the Simon Wiesenthal Center, a Jewish human rights organization. He has had his old tattoos removed so that he appears less like the thug he once was. Once a recruiter working to lure teenage boys into skinhead groups, he now works diligently to get them out. He knows of at least two dozen teens he has helped escape the hate lifestyle, and he feels good about that. Leyden states on his Web site, www.strhatetalk.com, "I want kids to realize that people are all human regardless of skin color, religion, sexual preference or whatever. Getting rid of a certain group will never happen first of all and will never take care of any one person's problem. Hate, violence, gangs, etc. will only create more havoc in our world today. I like to inspire and empower kids to look at the big picture, which was something I should have done."

Leyden's story of rebirth is compelling and hopeful, but the truth is that few ardent hatemongers ever go to work for the other side. Hate groups and those who oppose them remain locked in battle for the culture of America. As hate groups have grown in number and dangerousness, anti-hate groups have expanded their reach and activities to fight them.

The Ku Klux Klan in the 1920s

Glenn Feldman

Historians cite two major phases of Ku Klux Klan activity. The first was after the Civil War, and the second took place in the 1920s. The Klan was revived in the 1920s to increased membership and influence, and attempted to portray itself as a less terrifying entity. But the truth was that the Klan was still as hateful and malicious as always, and was still willing to use intimidation and violence against its targets. In the Klan of the 1920s, not only were African Americans victimized, but also immigrants, non-Protestants, and union workers. Particularly in the homogeneous area of Alabama, Klan activity reached its height.

In the following viewpoint Glenn Feldman reviews the growth of the Klan in the early twentieth century, its targets, and its activities. An author and historian, Feldman has written numerous articles and books on southern history and racial issues. He is an associate professor at the Center for Labor Education and Research at the University of Alabama–Birmingham.

The second Klan's attempt to regulate Alabama's societal morality derived much of its impetus from the order's exclusively Protestant orientation and a decidedly xenophobic impulse. It was a xenophobia broadly understood: a fear of things foreign that included people who were different racially, religiously, and ethnically as well as morally. The revised Klan thus shared something basic with its Reconstruction predecessor. Although World War I and 1919 clearly exacerbated xenophobic fears and thereby created a new situation and new imperatives for the second Klan, the basic urge to quash things foreign had roots at least as far back as the Reconstruction KKK and its campaign against freed blacks and Republicans of both colors. Much of the Reconstruction period in Alabama, and in the other southern states, involved efforts to recover political and social control from what were perceived as foreign and outside elements.

Targeting Victims Based on Race

By the turn of the century, race relations had sunk to new lows throughout the country. Atlanta experienced a race riot in 1906; two years later one occurred in the northern town of Springfield, Illinois. After 1900, lynching was reserved almost exclusively for blacks (during the 1890s in Alabama, one in every three lynch victims had been white). "Scientific racism" was generally accepted as wisdom. It acted as a positivist buttress that both reinforced and engendered racist attitudes and behaviors across the United States. Doctors, scientists, criminologists, statisticians, and psychologists north and south of the Mason-Dixon Line agreed that blacks were biologically "weaker," a burden to themselves and society because of their "simple minds," "primitive urges," and "lack of [sexual and moral] self-control." These attitudes found expression, not in the newsletters of racist groups on the lunatic fringe, but in respected and prestigious outlets such as the *American Journal of Psychiatry*, publications written by Cornell University faculty, and books sponsored by the American Economic Association.

Given the national complexion of racism, it is not surprising that there was violence and prejudice against blacks and other biologically "inferior" groups considered by science to be something less than human. Nor should it be shocking that whites, in the region where most blacks lived, moved toward disenfranchisement and rigid segregation once it was clear that the federal government meant to offer no obstacle. By the turn of the century, Henry Cabot Lodge's "force bill" had been defeated in the U.S. Senate. The U.S. Supreme Court, in a series of rulings, had declared that it intended to interpret the Fourteenth and Fifteenth Amendments in only the narrowest and least intrusive fashion. Meanwhile, the Spanish-American War and the annexation of Cuba, the Philippines, and the Sandwich Islands had led the nation as a whole, for the first time, to sympathize with the southern position on the racial question. The *Brooklyn Eagle*, for example, advocated repeal of the Fifteenth Amendment and black suffrage because, it reasoned, "human nature is a higher constitution than the Federal compact, . . . [and] White control is a better preservative of government and civilization than Constitutional amendments, which threaten to ignore or cross it." Disenfranchisement, the entrenchment of [the racist segregationism known as] Jim Crow, and, indeed, the founding of the Ku Klux Klan, took place within the warm and nurturing climate of sympathetic national opinion.

Like its precursors in Alabama, the revised KKK spent much time and energy defining its enemies. Like its earlier and later counterparts, too, the second Klan made African Americans its foremost enemy. [Klan revivalist William] Joseph Simmons led the way by defining white supremacy as an immutable doctrine dictated by nature. From his imperial headquarters in Atlanta, he urged Alabama Knights to preserve racial integrity from the "foul touch of a lower stock" and to keep Caucasian blood and civilization pure.

While southern Klansmen expressed considerable antipathy for Catholics, Jews, immigrants, and moral nonconformists, race was still central for most of them. In other sections of the country, Catholics received most of the Klan's attention, but in Alabama, and perhaps in much of the South, the race issue predominated. During the 1920s, southern blacks suffered—not to the extremes of Reconstruction—but still a great deal.

While Alabama Klansmen did attack whites—twelve in Birmingham alone in one four-month stretch—blacks were especially at risk. All kinds of behavior merited penalties. In Ensley, a mob flogged a black doctor for treating white female patients. Twelve Birmingham men beat a black porter for associating too closely with white women. Klansmen also made threats against the Alabama Power Company because blacks and whites were riding together on Montgomery's streetcars. City police denied that they had taken part in the masked beating of another Birmingham black despite evidence to the contrary.

Economic motivations played an important role in Alabama racism. Poor and working-class whites had long feared economic leveling with blacks. In fact, some historians have cited this fear as the single greatest factor retarding the ability of white folk to sustain a challenge to entrenched white power in the Black Belt and industrial cities of Alabama. During the 1920s, economic tensions persisted between average whites and blacks. In Selma, Klansmen who were most likely poor and working-class whites pressured blacks to give up their jobs in construction and farming. In 1924, Birmingham Klansmen lashed the white owner of a department store for hiring a black to head the carpet department. Another Jefferson County mob flogged a black for doing his factory job too well.

Klan Violence

In a fundamental sense that superseded even class, racist Klan violence mirrored the state as a whole. Lynching had been a virtual cottage industry in Alabama during the 1880s and 1890s. During the early 1900s, the number of lynch victims fell, but blacks were targeted more exclusively than ever before. African Americans habitually succumbed to other forms of violence as well. Alabama prison guards flogged black inmates so viciously that they sometimes died. Whites who associated too closely with blacks were also at risk. In 1921, a Birmingham mob mercilessly beat two men and a woman for being too friendly to blacks. City detectives dropped the case almost immediately—testimony to the closeness of the Klan's ties to the police.

Postwar racial tensions fueled much of the violence. In one 1919 spree, Montgomery vigilantes lynched four separate blacks in twelve hours. A pro-Klan grand jury refused to return any indictments, though, prompting Judge Leon Mc-Cord, a patrician, to speak out against the evils of hooded violence. McCord declared that although there had been an obvious need for the KKK during Reconstruction, "there is no need now for the Ku Klux."

During the first few years of the Klan's reincarnation, a trickle of such opposition to the order emanated from the business and legal communities, local governments, and civic associations; more came from Catholics, Jews, and northern critics. Alabama blacks, though, resisted the modern Klan from the moment of its revival in 1915. Blacks had been the primary victims of the original Klan's atrocities, and for many, the painful memory of those days lingered. The revised Klan made it clear that blacks were still enemy number one. Imperial Wizard Hiram Evans repeatedly told hooded audiences that "all good things" throughout history had come from the white race. NAACP leaders realized that the new Klan wanted to curb black voting, preserve and control black labor at low wages, and violate constitutionally guaranteed civil rights. In Birmingham, black newspapers cautioned their readers against being taken in by some of the more innocuous aspects of the new Klan. The main goal of the second Alabama Klan, they warned, as with its predecessor, was to ensure white supremacy at any cost. One black kidnap victim did more than merely warn others; he shot two masked Klansmen before escaping during a struggle over a pistol in the backseat of a car.

Alabama's revised KKK met virtually any gesture toward racial equality with violence and intimidation. In 1921, Mobile Knights warned black doctors that they had just three days to post the word "colored" on their shingles and stop treating white patients. Talladega mob members beat the president of the Alabama Negro Medical Association into senselessness, luring him from his home with a bogus emergency call. They left him to flounder in the woods for hours until an elderly white farmer helped him back to town. Two black ministers received mail bombs in 1921. Nine Klansmen visited the editorial offices of the black *Baptist Leader* and warned newsmen to stop printing criticism of the Klan. The KKK took out a full-page advertisement in the *Birmingham News* to oppose spending taxes on black schools and, on the same night, staged a 300-car parade and burned an enormous cross on the top of Red Mountain.

True crisis arrived in 1923 when federal officials announced that black physicians would begin working at Tuskegees's new veterans' hospital. Alabama Kluxers demonstrated their disapproval in a spectacular display that was backed by many others in the white community. Fifteen hundred Knights descended on Macon County to march, burn crosses, and intimidate the large black populace. Governor William "Plain Bill" Brandon asked the White House to help Alabamians keep the facility white. There was a thinly veiled threat of Klan violence against Robert R. Moton, the principal of the Tuskegee Institute, for siding with the black doctors, but he responded by threatening to lobby for a federal antilynching bill. Faced with this prospect, the elites backed down.

Flight, although the most common response by blacks, was itself dangerous. A Sheffield mob lynched two blacks in 1919 because they tried to flee north instead of staying to do farmwork for miserable wages in Shelby County. Near Grimes, a Houston County mob shot a black man as he waited on a platform for a train to take him north. In 1920, 800 Klansmen marched through Calhoun and Talladega Counties to intimidate blacks into staying in Alabama. Still, 400,000 blacks left the South during World War I, many in response to just such Klan actions. Louis Leibold of the *New York Herald* interviewed fleeing Alabama blacks and estimated that 25,000 had left the state after the war, mostly to seek better pay and to escape epidemic violence by the Klan. . . .

Targeting Immigrants

Recent immigrants were readily identifiable as outsiders in Alabama, foreigners who were put at risk by the pronouncements of Klan leaders like Hiram Evans. The imperial wizard described immigration as "poison" and told his minions that the "time has come when the villains who have . . . led their countries to despoliation" should not be allowed to emigrate to America. He also nativistically attacked Catholics and Jews, "masses of ignorant, superstitious, religious devotees."

Some Alabama Knights responded by terrorizing any immigrants they could find. Their activities in this regard overlapped with, and mimicked, those of a number of the patriotic societies associated with World War I. One masked Birmingham mob abducted the Rumanian owner of a confectionery and lashed him at gunpoint. Later, three hooded men flogged a German tailor and warned him to keep away from native women. In 1923, seventy-five Kluxers took part in a march through "Dago Town," the West Blocton section of Bibb County. On another occasion, in order to protest bootlegging, Kluxers burned a cross in Bibb County's "Little Italy," a poor area occupied by immigrant coal miners. Every Italian head of household armed himself and mustered in the town square to await a Klan attack, but it never came.

Alabama's religious, cultural, and ethnic homogeneity fueled such tendencies. In fact, 1920 Alabama was home to fewer than 18,000 immigrants, a mere 1.2 percent in a total population of 2.35 million. One-third of Alabama's sixty-seven counties, some with populations as large as 80,000, had fewer than 20 foreign-born residents.

Targeting Victims Based on Religion

The revised KKK also targeted Jews. Initially, Joseph Simmons claimed that his order was not anti-Semitic, only "pro-Christian." In 1923, Hiram Evans dropped pretenses when he declared that the assimilation of foreign Jews had given America colic and that Jews were conspiring to "set up Jewland in America." Reams of Klan propaganda denounced Jews for instigating racial tension, plotting to overthrow all "Gentile" governments, colluding with Communists, and controlling every newspaper in New York.

Anti-Semitism was quite prevalent among northern Knights, but Jews in Alabama also fell victim to the Klan in a number of ways. Irving Engel, a Birmingham attorney and later a Jewish leader of national repute, reluctantly moved to New York when he realized that Klan ascendance had made it almost impossible for him to win favorable verdicts in the city's courtrooms. Birmingham Knights burned crosses in front of Jewish homes, conspired to put Jewish-owned stores out of business, and had at least one Jewish comptroller fired. Talladega Kluxers boycotted Jewish-owned stores and ran one Jew out of town because he tried to marry a Protestant. Etowah County Klansmen terrorized a wealthy Jewish merchant until he surrendered the lease to his house and actually contributed money to the KKK....

Catholics also received attention from the revised KKK in Alabama during the 1920s, but in the state as a whole they were not persecuted more than other minorities. In Alabama, blacks remained the foremost Klan target. Still, during the 1920s anti-Catholicism was a strong new issue for the KKK. Joseph Simmons set the tone for his fellow Alabamians here, too, by denouncing Catholics as the explicit enemies of his new organization. As in his references to Jews, Simmons refused to admit that his order was "anti-Catholic," preferring the euphemism "pro-Protestant." The Alabamian Hiram Evans, who was his successor, and official Klan propaganda, were more blunt. They accused the Pope of making secret treaties to bring on World War I, of opposing republican forms of government, of controlling the press, and of stockpiling arms for an imminent Catholic takeover of Washington. Klaverns sponsored female lecturers posing as "escaped nuns" to relate ghastly tales about the carnal lust of priests and the evils of parochial education. The "nuns" displayed leather bags, which Catholics supposedly used to cremate the infant products of priest and nun sexual unions in the basement furnaces of their churches.

Anti-Catholic rhetoric translated into specific acts of violence, intimidation, and bigotry at the local level. When Alabama Klansmen were able to lay their hands on Alabama's few Catholics, they often did so. In 1916, hooded Knights sent shock waves through Birmingham's small Catholic community by burning the Catholic church and school at Pratt City. Klansmen also encouraged people to boycott stores with Catholic owners or employees, pressured businesses to fire their Catholic employees, and protested the construction of at least one church simply because it was Catholic.

Birmingham's 1917 city elections were particularly marred by anti-Catholic prejudice. Five city commissioners were elected with the strong support of the True Americans, a group prominent during World War I that repudiated Catholics, Jews, and other "foreign elements" in American society. In the race for the commission presidency, a physician in East Lake defeated the Episcopalian incumbent largely by accusing him of being a "tool of the Roman Catholic Church." In the midst of the campaign, Sidney J. Catts, a Baptist preacher and the governor of Florida, came to Birmingham to warn of the Catholic menace. A number of local Protestants swapped stories about the sexual immorality of Catholic clergy, stockpiled arms, and uttered prohibitions against lay reading of the Bible.

In 1919 Thomas E. Kilby won the governorship largely by appealing to trenchant anti-Catholicism among his fellow Alabamians. Two years later, a Birmingham jury dominated by Klansmen acquitted a Knight who had confessed to killing a priest in broad daylight. In 1921, Governor Kilby fired his popular state police chief for conducting unauthorized liquor raids in Mobile. The underlying issue for many, however, was the Catholic faith and culture. One Mobile Protestant blamed the firing on the city's wet Catholic populace, "the people doing all they can to destroy our public schools and Protestantism from the world." "You have simply disgraced our Protestant Church," he informed the governor. "Never has there been such a frame-up of dirty Catholics and whiskey-heads before. I am tired of seeing my people treated by this horde of foreigners as if we were human dogs. . . . We are on the eve of a revolution in this country."

The Klan fed on such narrow cultural and sectarian prejudice. On one occasion, twelve sheeted Mobile Knights raided a Catholic convent and playground, terrorizing a number of small children, who mistook them for ghosts. Soon after the raid, two brothers burned a Klan cross in front of a Catholic church at nearby Oakdale while services were under way inside. Kluxers burned five other crosses in Mobile on the same night in what smacked of an organized campaign of terror.

The American Neo-Nazi Movement in the Late Twentieth Century

Elinor Langer

In the past, hate groups developed individually having their own motivations, hierarchies, and activities. Toward the end of the twentieth century, however, more hate groups joined efforts to attack shared targets. This development makes modern hate groups more complicated and more dangerous. Not only are they potentially more powerful and widespread, but they influence each other and thus broaden their hatred. Analysts who follow hate groups and their crimes warn Americans not to be lulled into a false sense of complacency by believing that the days of white supremacism, anti-Semitism, and other hate ideologies are gone. Instead, hate crimes may continue to become more difficult to pin on particular groups, making them more difficult to neutralize.

Author and journalist Elinor Langer writes and speaks about the rise of neo-Nazism in America and what can be done to combat it. In this viewpoint, she discusses the murder of an Ethiopian man at the hands of three skinheads. She expanded this topic to book length with A Hundred Little Hitlers: The Death of a Black Man, the Trial of a White Racist, and the Rise of the Neo-Nazi Movement in America.

I live in Portland, Oregon, where in November 1988 three skinheads murdered an Ethiopian man, and like many of my friends and neighbors, I was startled to see how—literally—close to home it had come. The murder took place in a

Elinor Langer, "The American Neo-Nazi Movement Today," *The Nation*, vol. 251, No. 3, July 16–23, 1990, pp. 82–107. Reprinted by permission of Georges Borchardt, Inc., on behalf of the author.

neighborhood very near where my husband and I had lived when we first moved to Portland years before. Of the three assailants, one was a neighbor living a few blocks away in a building in which I had just considered taking an office; the second was a rock musician and all-round counterculture personage who moved in circles close to those of our baby sitter as well as, at some points, close to mine; and the third was a recent homecoming king of a local high school with some of whose friends and schoolmates my own acquaintances also overlapped.

Originally, the boys were to have been tried jointly and, my attention having been caught, I arranged to write about the trial for [the *Nation*]. It then transpired that the cases were severed, and ultimately, because the defendants all pleaded guilty, there were no trials at all. But in the meantime, as you will see, the trail had led directly from the Portland skinheads, members of a local gang called East Side White Pride, to a California-based neo-Nazi organization called White Aryan Resistance (WAR) and to its youth arm, the Aryan Youth Movement (AYM), headed, respectively, by a man named Tom Metzger and his son, John, and my article on the Portland case had become [a] special issue of the *Nation* on the movement as a whole.

Challenges of Studying Neo-Nazism

In introducing to *Nation* readers a subject that until recently I knew little about, I feel a certain diffidence; my chief comfort in doing so is that one of the things I have realized during this period is how little is generally known. Unlikely as it seems, there appears to be only a handful of scholars at work on specialized aspects of the movement, and as far as I have been able to learn there is no ongoing research of a general sociological nature. The books that are available have been written mostly by journalists, invariably as a result of having

95

covered some local occurrence, but these, though useful, tend to suffer from an excess of anecdote and an absence of documentation. There are organizations that at first glance appear to know everything and without which no one looking at the neo-Nazi movement would get very far, but their interests also are specialized, and it soon becomes apparent that though their facts are indispensable their assumptions are arguable, and it is necessary to weigh their interpretations against one's own.

In writing about a subject that carries with it the automatic weight of its association with Nazi Germany, I find myself uncomfortable for another reason, suspended between caution and alarm. Especially about a movement as underreported as this one, you do not write, in the first place, merely to observe "This too will pass away"; you write to sound an alert. At the same time, you know that the tests of time are different and that historians of another generation will consider the evidence and say either that it was all simply part of another "Brown Scare" in which people, as usual, lost their heads, and some their civil liberties, or that a dangerous movement was on the rise and that we failed to discern it early enough and help stamp it out. I do not know where along that spectrum the truth of the neo-Nazi movement lies. I do know that it is among us, that it is violent and mean, and that it is time to open up the subject for further investigation and discussion so that out of a broader base of information and a variety of perspectives there can possibly be fashioned a sound response.

In using the term *neo-Nazi*, I am referring roughly to an array of groups and individuals, including:

- Nazis: old-line groups principally descended from the American Nazi Party founded by George Lincoln Rockwell in 1959, whose members still appear in uniform, as well as other small Nazi-identified parties and groupings whose members usually do not.

- The skinheads: youth gangs in various cities with names like Youth of Hitler and the Confederate Hammerskinssome, like San Francisco's American Front, openly connected with Metzger's WAR, and some not; skinheads are the fastest-growing wing of the movement today.

- The Ku Klux Klan: no longer the centralized Klan of previous eras, but three separate and rival Klan federations and innumerable splinter groups; it is a government-infiltrated and at times government-manipulated Klan, a shadow of its former self, many of whose units are, however, "Nazified" in that they cooperate freely with the Nazi groups (something that was unthinkable in the past, when the Klan's patriotism and the Nazis' Germanophilism invariably clashed) and share many of the same ideas.

- The Posse Comitatus: a decentralized, antistate and largely rural movement, which also appears as the Christian Patriots or American Freemen Association, whose adherents believe, among other things, that all government should be rooted at the county level and that cooperating with any higher authority, including the IRS [Internal Revenue Service] or, indeed, even the state Department of Motor Vehicles, is wrong.

- The Christian Identity movement: an Aryan-inspired religious denomination descended from a nineteenth-century movement known as Anglo-Israelism or British Israelism, which holds that the "chosen people" of the Bible are white Anglo-Saxons, that Jews are descended from Satan and that all nonwhites are "pre-Adamic" "mud people" a lower species than whites; it is a religious movement that, as in the case of Idaho's Aryan Nations–Church of Jesus Christ, Christian (as opposed to Jesus Christ, Jew), is often indistinguishable from a political one.

Hate Groups in Collaboration

In the phrase "neo-Nazi movement", both the terms "neo-Nazi" and "movement" require further discussion, and they have to be argued together. [A map] recently issued by the Klanwatch Project of the Southern Poverty Law Center (SPLC) in Montgomery, Alabama, . . . includes the categories listed above, [but] it uses the overall heading "white supremacist" and reserves "neo-Nazi" for the groups that had their genesis with Rockwell. The term "white supremacist" is also used by another major monitoring organization, the Center for Democratic Renewal in Atlanta. The problem with this usage, it seems to me, is not that it is wrong but that it does not go far enough, retaining an old-fashioned, unduly Southern and narrowly political flavor that fails to reflect the modern racialism that comes to us directly from the Nazi era and that I think is the essential characteristic these groups share. The neo-Nazi label does have varying degrees of applicability. James Farrands, Imperial Wizard of The Invisible Empire, Knights of the Ku Klux Klan, with whom I [once] spoke, was indignant at being associated with neo-Nazis and at pains to assure me that "you don't have to be a Nazi to be an anti-semite," and to find a member of the Posse Comitatus with the same revulsion would not be difficult. But for the most part these organizations have no enemies to the right. If there are those within the movement who object to their Nazi bedfellows, they do not generally make themselves heard.

More important than any differences among the groups is the fact that the individuals within them function together as a movement and know that they are one—a point on which the two monitoring organizations mentioned above, as well as the Anti-Defamation League of B'nai B'rith (ADL), largely agree. . .

Quantifying the Problem

The reader would undoubtedly like to know how many people are involved, a point on which the available data are unfortunately not very good. Estimates made [in 1990] by the three monitoring organizations mentioned above range from about 10,000 to about 20,000 members of these groups nationally, with the organizations agreeing on a rule of thumb of about ten passive supporters for every hard-core member—and thus a possible total of up to 200,000—and agreeing as well that the numbers are conservative. The larger number, which by some counts includes an additional 30,000 Christian Identity followers, is also presumed to include the 100,000 or so subscribers to a Washington, D.C.–based newspaper called the *Spotlight*, published by an ideologically similar but stylistically dissimilar far-right organization, the Liberty Lobby, founded in 1957 by Willis Carto, who also founded the revisionist Institute for Historical Review and the contemporary Populist Party, as well as the 44,000 people who voted for the 1988 Populist presidential candidate, David Duke.

As uncertain as the number of adherents is the number of incidents of hate-motivated violence that we read about in our papers every day; everyone agrees they are dramatically increasing, but there are no reliable figures. With the exception of the ADL, which issues an annual audit of anti-semitic incidents (1,432 in 1989, a 12 percent increase over the previous year), most national organizations prefer not to quantify, believing that with the violence and the reporting apparently increasing simultaneously, the situation is not only a social but also a statistical mess; and with a monitoring agency in the Northwest alone reporting a 400 percent overall increase during the same year, this seems a reasonable inference. The Hate Crimes Statistics Act signed [April 23, 1990,] by President [George H. W.] Bush requires the Justice Department to begin keeping national statistics for the first time, but since participation by state and local police agencies is voluntary—and certain acts, such as cross burnings, may in some cases be arbitrarily excluded—it is questionable how comprehensive they will be.

More important than the number either of members or of incidents, however, is the relationship between the two—a matter that has scarcely begun to be discussed. While it appears that most hate crimes are committed by individuals who are not associated with any organized group, the impulses of the member and the nonmember appear to be much the same. If it is an exaggeration to say that every hate criminal is a potential neo-Nazi, certainly they give the leaders reason to hope. At the least, there appears to be a kind of multiplier effect whereby one thing leads to another, and the mere existence of the movement acts as an enabling force for the open expressions of racism that, until recently, have tended to be underground. There is a dynamism at work here that any static accounting, whether of "members" or "incidents" cannot reflect. Tom Metzger is one of the principal sources of that dynamism. . . .

The Murder of Seraw in Portland

At 1:30 on the morning of November 13, 1988, in a peaceful residential neighborhood in Portland, Oregon, Kenneth Mieske, Kyle Brewster and Steven Strasser, skinheads, encountered Mulageta Seraw, Wondwosen Tesfaye and Tilahun Antneh, Ethiopians; the skinheads had a bat; and Seraw—the description of whose wounds makes chilling reading—died. The contents of the skinheads' apartments, searched shortly afterward, make equally chilling reading—bats and clubs in one, the latest racial propaganda in another, a veritable library on the rise and fall of the Third Reich in the third—all used by the district attorneys to prove what, from the moment the police first arrived at the scene, hardly anyone besides other skinheads has ever doubted: that it was a racially motivated attack and not a street fight that got out of hand and brought about the death of Mulageta Seraw.

The Portland story is worth examining because both locally and nationally it marked the beginning of a new realization that when you see a bunch of black-jacketed, heavy-booted storm troopers on TV, you might not be watching a World War II film; it could be the evening news. The three skinheads are in prison—Mieske, who pleaded guilty to murder, for a minimum of twenty years; Brewster and Strasser, who pleaded guilty to manslaughter, for a minimum of ten and nine years, respectively—but the case has acquired symbolic status, and neither within the neo-Nazi movement nor among its opponents has it been forgotten. . . .

Hate Movement in Portland

The clearest marker for the emergence of the skinheads from the [punk music] clubs to the streets is probably early 1988, when ideological links between such acts as the desecration of a synagogue and an attack on a homosexual couple led police to begin keeping records:

- "Black male victim is assaulted and called 'nigger' and 'jungle bunny' by three members of Youth of Hitler."

- "Business was burglarized and vandalized. The suspect painted 'Nazi Rule, White Power, Die No Name Jew, Die Nigger Lover, White Rule.'"

- "A note saying 'Niggers get out' was left on a WF's [white female's] car parked in front of her home. The WF claimed to have seen skinheads in the area and is willing to press charges. She is dating a BM [black male] and felt the note to be specific harassment."

On March 10, 1988, an event occurred that for the first time focused public attention on what was happening in the streets. HockSeng (Sam) Chin, a native of Singapore married to a white woman, was leaving a Thai restaurant in downtown Portland with his wife and child when he was set upon by three skinheads who shouted, "Go back to Hong Kong" and "Get out of our country," called his daughter a "f--king slant" and denounced his wife as a "race traitor" for being married to someone nonwhite. Portland police have had their own collisions with minorities at times, but when one of the skinheads continued his tirade even after his arrest by insisting that the United States should exclude Asian visitors and trade, it was clearly too much. "I suggested before he talked about business & trade maybe he should get an education" notes the arresting officer's report. Concern about this and other skinhead incidents, initially confined to the police, was soon widely shared. Coverage in the daily *Oregonian* increased, and in mid-May a lengthy article in *Willamette Week* took a close look at a neo-Nazi skinhead gang called POWAR (Preservation of the White American Race). Shortly afterward members of the gang appeared live on the Sunday evening TV show *Town Hall*, a program of the ABC affiliate KATU-TV and an important local forum.

The *Town Hall* program deserves special attention, for unlike its national counterparts it features real discussion, and it represented a largely sincere attempt on the part of the skins to communicate with the public in a reasonable fashion. It occurred nearly half a year before Seraw's murder, and may also suggest something of the state of mind of skinheads in other areas where organizing by a sophisticated national leadership has not taken place. Pressed by the moderator to explain themselves, the dozen or so skins produced a stumbling but plainly heartfelt array of statements—"I'm standing up for what I believe in, fighting for a cause"; "we're trying to unite the white people"; "we want our culture to still be here for future generations, we don't want to lose it"; "today we have a lot of black history, African history, things like that, but no awareness of what it means to be white; we're human too."—that in the confrontational atmosphere of Geraldo or Oprah would have sounded deliberately provocative or else rhetorical, but which here became the expressions of an uncertain sense of cultural and individual identity.

The program's most intense moments came as a result of a demand by the president of Portland's police union, not noted for his liberal views, to know just what role Nazi ideology played in the POWAR organization. "A cause is one thing" he said, shaking with a palpably generational rage, "but these young people weren't even around when [World War II was fought]. . . . In a local newspaper they had a picture of this young lad here standing next to a swastika. . . . Now to have that swastika hanging on the wall next to an American flag is a damned insult. . . . There's a lot of white people that were killed in that war, not necessarily blacks or Asians or Jews as the case may be; they were just a lot of American soldiers regardless of race killed in that damn war, and if [the skinheads] have adopted the philosophy of the Gestapo kind of people, they've adopted a very dangerous philosophy." Taken up by the moderator, who itemized the militaria in the photo in question, including a Nazi battlefield flag with the Iron Cross, a Hitler T-shirt worn by a skin who was also on the program, the death's head symbol of the S.S. and various swastikas, the inventory elicited responses from several skinheads on the program.

- Kelly, a handsome, soft-spoken young man who was POWAR's more or less official spokesman, said: "There are various symbols of the white man's attempt to be pure: the swastika, the Rebel flag and so on. We do not support the Third Reich attitudes for, say, genocide or the mass extermination of a certain race in any way."

- Michelle, a 21-year-old heavily tattooed woman, who noted that she had been a skin for about five years, said: "I don't agree with those philosophies in the sense of violence and extermination but there are philosophies from that era that we all claim as having something to do with the preservation of the white race. We've taken something from the past and fine-tuned it toward the future!"

- John, a younger skin from Salem, Oregon, said: "O.K., at that point our country was divided. Half of our country was for Germany and half of our country was for England. Because of our President, we went with England. If it hadn't happened that way, who's to say if it would be immoral for us to have a swastika beside an American flag?"

- "So you're saying the country was half-divided?" asked the astonished moderator. "Do you recall the vote in Congress to declare war on Germany? It was 535 to 1!"

- "Yes, but that was because of the beliefs of our Congress, who was in office at that time," replied John from Salem. . . .

Portland After Seraw's Murder

Since the death of Seraw, skinhead activity in Portland has only intensified. Not only have the number of individual hate crimes attributed to skinheads and other white supremacists continued to increase but antiracist skin gangs have also emerged, encouraged in part by the San Francisco–based, leftist John Brown Anti-Klan Committee, in part by the militant Portland Coalition for Human Dignity, and confrontations are escalating. Fights between gangs of skinheads and gangs of blacks are also being reported. Tom Metzger has gained prominence, maintaining two Portland message lines where previously he had none, speaking with the press and on talk shows in connection with the lawsuit and generally keeping moving.

Trying to Explain Modern Racial Violence and Hate

Attempting to account for the skinhead phenomenon nationally, some observers have arrived at the usual explanations— inadequate economic opportunity, individual pathology and broken homes—that, for Portland at least, appear to me to be insufficient. Although it is true that today's skinheads are members of the first generation that cannot expect to make more money than its parents, which undoubtedly plays a part, they are young, many still live at home, and they do not appear to worry about money much. They come from every suburb, wealthy to working-class, and from an array of families whose "functionality" or "dysfunctionality" appears to be no different from that of the people next door. As for individual pathology, even in the case of Kenneth Mieske, who wielded the bat that killed Seraw, opposing psychologists for the prosecution and defense said, respectively, "He has an interesting psychological profile which does not indicate the presence of serious psychological problems" and "I would not characterize him as showing a personality disorder"—though whether that is more of a commentary on Mieske or on the psychologists is hard to say.

My own look at the Portland skinheads suggests, rather, an acute degree of painfully personal racial discomfort, which is finding its natural expression in a primitive political movement. Comparing the Portland of his youth with the Portland of today, a skinhead in his mid-20s sounded almost plaintive as he explained that "Portland isn't safe anymore and it's never going to get better; it will never be the same." Another said he didn't mind if black people went everywhere and did everything they wanted, but sometimes he and his friends just liked to be alone. Closely entwined with a sense of loss is a sense of fear. The middle class girl driving the car in which the skinheads involved in the Seraw murder were riding was carrying a gun given to her by her father for protection. The mother of one skinhead, upon pressing her son to explain the weapons that are part of his uniform, got a desperate, "Ma, you just don't understand." Not only do Portland skinheads I talked to cite black gangs as the crucial factor in their own gang formation, but their anxiety is so free-floating that those in attendance at bail hearings for the Seraw case—including

105

one of the passengers in the car—claim to have thought that not just the Ethiopians in the car with Seraw but even, at one point, a black observer in the courtroom, was either a Crip or a Blood. Whether the sense of intimidation felt by young whites is associated with any substantive improvements for blacks in Portland, it is not possible to say, but it is true that, like many cities, Portland has, in the lifetime of this generation, changed from an informally segregated city to an open one; that schools, parks, bus stops and malls once divided are now used by all; and that the resulting encounters between young people of different races at times and places adults rarely tread have left a wake of ill feeling that the city's predominantly liberal political establishment has been slow to acknowledge.

To what extent the skinhead movement is simply a punk version of racism elsewhere in the city and not a separable phenomenon is another question that has not been adequately discussed, but certainly the case could easily be made. Throughout the city, crimes of the sort formerly committed largely by skinheads are now frequently committed by other white supremacists as well, and while the children have been in the streets, adults have been engaged in a subtler but no less ugly struggle against the renaming of a city thoroughfare for Martin Luther King Jr. This campaign has not only resurrected the political careers of two long-term leaders of the right in Oregon, Walter and Rosalie Huss, but has brought to the city such racist leaders as Richard Barrett, head of the Mississippi-based Nationalist Movement, who before the Seraw murder usually stayed away. In these circumstances, to attribute the disturbances in Portland or any other city to Tom Metzger is like attributing the civil rights movement to outside agitators. Wherever he can find a forum, Metzger operates, but he does not create the conditions in which his words make sense. From individual white insecurity to a collective white identity; from a collective white identity to the necessity of white supremacy; and from the necessity of white supremacy to the movement for Aryan victory, with all that it implies—it is on this classic political journey from experience to ideology that Tom Metzger, among others, is attempting to lead the skinheads, but before they ever encountered him, the experience was already there.

Major Anti-Hate Groups

Kendal Broad and Valerie Jenness

Along with the rise of hate groups has come the rise of groups whose mission is combating them. Some are religious and some are secular, but they all seek to educate and advocate as means to diminish the activities of hate groups. Among the most prominent anti-hate groups are the Anti-Defamation League, the National Institute Against Prejudice and Violence, the Center for Democratic Renewal, the Southern Poverty Law Center, the National Gay and Lesbian Task Force, the National Coalition Against Domestic Violence, and the National Victim Center. Some of these groups focus on particular victim groups, while others provide support for anyone targeted for hate crimes. Further, some groups focus their efforts in a specific area such as law or education. Regardless, they are all committed to wiping out hate groups and their criminal activities.

Valerie Jenness and Kendal Broad in the following viewpoint provide brief overviews of the major anti-hate groups and their missions. Jenness has written extensively on the subject of law and human rights. She is a professor of criminology, law, and society at the University of California–Irvine. Like Jenness, Broad's interests are in social change, gender and minority issues, and social deviance. She is an associate professor of sociology and women's studies at the University of Florida.

Consistent with the foci of the modern civil rights movement, the contemporary women's movement, the gay and lesbian movement, and the crime victim movement in the United States, beginning in the late 1960s and continuing into the present era, a plethora of organizations have emerged to

Kendal Broad and Valerie Jenness, *Hate Crimes: New Social Movements and the Politics of Violence*, Hawthorne, NY: Aldine de Gruyter, 1997, pp. 31–46. Copyright © 1997 by Aldine Publishers. Reprinted by permission of AldineTransaction, a division of Transaction Publishers.

bring attention to and curb violence directed at minority constituencies. In the latter part of the twentieth century, watchdog organizations have emerged at the national, regional, state, and local levels to play a key role in documenting instances of violence that target minority members of the community, identifying and publicizing harm associated with bias-motivated violence, submitting proposals for reform, calling on the law to intervene on behalf of select injured constituencies, and providing social services to victims of bias-motivated violence. In the process, these organizations have collectively redefined age-old conduct and constructed new portraits of victimization.

A brief description of seven of the larger, more established, and pivotal antiviolence organizations . . . demonstrates how these types of organizations have proceeded to play a decisive role in the politics of violence. Specifically, the following seven organizations have emerged to engage in activism that brings newfound attention to hate-motivated violence. At the same time, they promote the interests of select constituencies by demanding changes in public policy, including the law. The description that follows is not meant to provide a comprehensive overview; rather, it is presented to illustrate the way in which various organizations emerged and responded to what they perceive to be an escalation of racial, ethnic, religious, and other forms of intergroup conflict.

The Anti-Defamation League of B'nai B'rith

As the most established antiviolence organization in the United States, the Anti-Defamation League of B'nai B'rith (ADL) was founded in 1969. Since then, it has been concerned with many types of bias crime, but its primary focus is on anti-Semitic violence. Since 1979 the ADL has been tracking anti-Semitic violence and has periodically published an annual Audit of Anti-Semitic Incidents. Based on data reported to ADL regional offices around the nation, these reports describe various "acts of harassment, threat and assault against individuals, their property and their institutions" and reveal a substantial increase in reported anti-Semitic vandalism and violence from year to year. In addition to the *Audit of Anti-Semitic Incidents*, the ADL produces and disseminates other publications on the nature of bias-motivated violence. For example, in 1982 the first edition of *Hate Groups in America* was released. In response to the findings documented in these types of publications, the ADL's counteraction program has been devoted to heightening media exposure, establishing and sustaining education programs, demanding more effective law enforcement, and actively supporting new legislation designed to combat anti-Semitic and racist violence. In 1981 the ADL's Legal Affairs Department drafted a model hate crime bill to be introduced in state legislatures. Like other lesser-known organizations, including many civil rights groups, the ADL's work has underscored the victim status of those harmed by violence *because* of their race and/or religion.

The National Institute Against Prejudice and Violence

Like the ADL, the National Institute Against Prejudice & Violence (NIAPV) in Baltimore, Maryland, has focused on what is now termed "ethnoviolence." Comprised of acts that are motivated by racial, religious, or ethnic prejudice, ethnoviolence includes physical assaults, verbal harassment, attacks on people's homes, and various forms of vandalism. As a letter to their members described:

> While other organizations deal with select aspects of prejudice and violence, the Institute is unique in its comprehensive approach. We act as a clearinghouse of information on reported incidents of intergroup conflict; study the effects of victimization; track the quantity and quality of news media activity; publish reports and educational materials; provide training, education, and consultation within communities;

and work with lawmakers advising on appropriate state and federal legislative remedies.

Since its founding in 1984, the NIAPV has published and made available to the public over fifteen documents, including *Striking Back at Bigotry: Remedies under Federal and State Law for Violence Motivated by Racial, Religious, or Ethnic Prejudice* [1991]. This document inventories the criminal and civil remedies available under federal and state law for violence motivated by racial, religious, and ethnic hatred. It is intended primarily to inform victims of these crimes and their attorneys of the various avenues of legal recourse against offenders of bias crime; the goal is to enable attorneys and their clients to arrive at the most effective combination of legal remedies to fully vindicate the victims' rights. As an NIAPV membership letter declared, "[C]entral to all of our work is our own motivation to help people break free of the norms of denial and the culture of silence that has characterized intergroup relations in the U.S. through its history."

The Center for Democratic Renewal

Founded in 1979, the Center for Democratic Renewal (CDR), formerly known as the National Anti-Klan Network, is an Atlanta-based antiracist organization with offices in Kansas City and Seattle. According to its bimonthly newsletter the *Monitor*, the CDR is "leading the fight against bigoted violence and hate group activity in America today. The CDR is a multi-racial, multi-ethnic, interfaith, non-profit organization dedicated to promoting constructive non-violent responses to hate violence and the white supremacist movement." Like the ADL and the NIAPV, the CDR acts as a national clearinghouse for efforts to counter hate group activity and bigoted violence through public education, community response, leadership training, and research. The CDR has been primarily concerned with monitoring and addressing antiracist violence associated with the Ku Klux Klan (KKK). In addition to tracking the organization and activities of the KKK, the CDR has collected data on bias-motivated violence and has sought legal and extralegal redress in light of their discoveries. Although the CDR's original focus was on racist violence, over the years it has developed a much broader agenda. Like the ADL and the NIAPV, the CDR's purview currently includes violence motivated by bigotry and directed at homosexuals. By broadening their agenda over the years, these organizations have expanded the domain of victim status to include violence against gays and lesbians.

The Southern Poverty Law Center

As a nonprofit foundation supported by private donations, the Southern Poverty Law Center (SPLC) in Montgomery, Alabama, was founded in 1971. The SPLC's Klanwatch Project was established in 1980 to address racist violence through litigation, education, and monitoring. Since then, the SPLC's Klanwatch Project continues to operate as a private intelligence agency. It collects data on the KKK and other white supremacist groups and sustains one of the most complete lists of hate groups and hate leaders in the United States; compiles perpetration and victimization data based on police and news sources; and pursues legal redress by bringing lawsuits against members of the Klan's Invisible Empire in Alabama, Texas, North Carolina, and Georgia. While the Klanwatch Project primarily focuses on racist violence, it nonetheless acknowledges the importance of devoting attention to antigay and lesbian violence, Indeed, the Klanwatch Project uses the term "hate violence" to refer to "crimes committed by whites against minorities, Jews, and gays where there is evidence of bias motivation."

The National Gay and Lesbian Task Force

The National Gay and Lesbian Task Force (NGLTF) was founded in Washington, D.C., in 1973 to promote the interests of gays and lesbians in the United States. As a civil rights organization representing the interests of gays and lesbians in the United States, the NGLTF has over 17,000 members and houses various projects, including the Privacy/Civil Rights Project, the Lesbian and Gay Families Project, the Campus Organizing Project, and the Anti-Violence Project. The NGLTF's Anti-Violence Project was established in 1982 to contribute to the overall goals of the NGLTF, including the specific civil rights and social change goals articulated by other divisions within the NGLTF.

The NGLTF's Anti-Violence Project devotes attention to promoting an appropriate official response to antigay violence, improving the treatment of lesbians and gay men by the criminal justice system, and assisting local communities in organizing against prejudice and violence. By using a combination of incident reports and survey research, the NGLTF's Anti-Violence Project has been collecting data since 1984. These data are reported in publications like *Anti-Gay Violence, Victimization and Defamation in 1987* and *Anti-Gay/Lesbian Violence, Victimization & Defamation in 1990*. In addition to sustaining data collection efforts, the NGLTF continues to pursue legal redress for violence directed at gays and lesbians.

The National Coalition Against Domestic Violence

The National Coalition Against Domestic Violence (NCADV) was formally organized in 1978 when over 100 battered-women's advocates from all parts of the nation attended the U.S. Commission on Civil Rights' hearing in Washington, D.C. on battered women. The NCADV [as of the late 1990s] has members from over two thousand programs in over eighty thousand cities across the United States. Governed by a working board of directors comprised of women from all over the country and representatives of task forces, who are themselves active in domestic violence programs in their communities,

113

the NCADV's mission is to offer assistance with common problems faced by programs operating in isolation at the local level. . . .

The National Victim Center

According to [Frank] Weed, "the founding of [the National Organization of Victim Assistance] in 1975 is an outgrowth of a perceived need by people working within crime victim programs who attended two conferences sponsored by the Department of Justice's Law Enforcement Assistance Agency (LEAA)". The need was twofold: (1) to provide coordination and communication between smaller regional and local programs without threatening their autonomy, and (2) to provide leadership at the national level, especially in terms of pursuing agreed-upon legislation. As Weed describes:

> The founding of the National Organization of Victim Assistance (NOVA) in 1975, and a decade later the National Victim Center (NVC), helped provide a larger focus to the efforts of thousands of grassroots crime victims' groups that address the specialized concerns of particular crime victims.

To accomplish this, the NVC serves as a national resource for over eight thousand organizations and many thousands of individuals each year.

As a nonprofit organization, the NVC engages in a number of activities designed to reduce the consequences of crime on victims. Most notably, the NVC (1) compiles statistics and produces a national report, which is then made available to libraries, governmental agencies, and political organizations across the United States; (2) publishes the journal *Victimology*, which is also distributed to libraries, governmental agencies, and political organizations across the United States; (3) engages in legal advocacy at the state and national level in order to protect and restore the rights of crime victims; (4) raises funds to support programs and efforts across the country; and

(5) sponsors educational efforts designed to make citizens, law enforcement officials, crime victims, and offenders aware of the rights of victims. As a [1993] *National Victim Center Annual Report* summarized:

Our goal is to raise the consciousness of the entire nation with a powerful message: Victims are not to blame for the crimes committed against them. They deserve rights in the criminal justice system and services and programs to aid in their painful recovery.

This message is, of course, one that all of the organizations and social movements described in this [viewpoint] embrace and promote.

CHAPTER 3

Legislating Against Hate

Chapter Preface

Although hate crime has been around as long as civilization itself, legislation to address the problem is a fairly recent development. Even the term "hate crime" was not popularized until 1988, when advocates deemed the existing term "bias crime" too bland. "Hate crime," they felt, better captured the passionate and detestable nature of the crimes and their perpetrators. While the first hate crime laws were pursued—and sometimes passed—to protect African Americans and Jews, laws today are in place to protect all ethnicities and religions, people with physical or mental disabilities, people of all sexual orientations, and women.

In the United States, the first federal law including language about hate crime did not come along until 1968's Civil Rights Act. At the state level, the first law was passed in Massachusetts in 1979. In 1990, the Hate Crimes Statistics Act was passed to require the Department of Justice to capture and summarize data related to hate crimes.

In 1997, the first run at passing the Hate Crimes Prevention Act was made. It did not pass. The bill was reintroduced in 1999, when it again failed to pass. The text of this bill states that hate crimes are not adequately addressed under existing legislation. Given that not all states have enacted their own hate crime legislation, advocates feel it is appropriate that measures be taken at a federal level. The bill, which places women, gays and lesbians, and the disabled under its protective umbrella, calls for specific penalties for those convicted of hate crimes. Without this legislation, federal prosecutors could only pursue a hate crime case if the victim was involved in a federal matter, such as voting, at the time of the attack. And if a state has no hate crime laws, or vague ones, without the Hate Crimes Prevention Act federal prosecutors have no grounds to intervene. In 2003 language was added to the bill, calling for stiffer penalties for those convicted of hate crimes. The bill even includes language regarding adults who recruit juveniles into hate crime activities. Adults found guilty of such recruitment could face enhanced penalties in addition to the consequences of involving a minor in a crime.

The Hate Crimes Prevention Act remains locked in legislative limbo as of 2007, the subject of debate among politicians, policy makers, and citizens. People are extremely divided on the matter of whether or not hate crimes deserve special status and whether stricter penalties serve as a deterrent to those poised to commit such crimes.

An Overview of State and Federal Legislation

Ryken Grattet and Valerie Jenness

The issue of hate-crime legislation is complicated by the fact that some policies are considered at the federal level, while some are considered at the state level. Policy makers have struggled to determine to what extent, if any, hate crime should be a matter for legislation. In the late twentieth century, there was a heightened demand for such laws, which resulted in the passage of more hate-crime laws at both levels. Almost all states have hate-crime laws, although the language and breadth of them varies. At the federal level, laws such as the Hate Crimes Statistics Act, the Violence Against Women Act, and the Hate Crimes Sentencing Enhancement Act all address the unique issues of hate crimes and their perpetrators.

In the following excerpt, Ryken Grattet and Valerie Jenness summarize the scope of state and federal legislation regarding hate crimes. Grattet is an associate professor of sociology at the University of California–Davis. Jenness is a professor of criminology, law, and society at the University of California–Irvine. Both have written individually and collaboratively on legal issues pertaining to human rights.

Although anyone is potentially a victim of crime, some groups are particularly susceptible to victimization because of their vulnerability, social marginality, or [social] invisibility. Some criminals use a victim's minority group membership as a means of gauging the victim's level of guardianship and the degree to which society cares about what happens to

Ryken Grattet and Valerie Jenness, "Examining the Boundaries of Hate Crime Law: Disabilities and the 'Dilemma of Difference,'" *Journal of Criminal Law and Criminology*, vol. 91, No. 3, 2001, p. 653–98. Copyright © 2001 by Northwestern University, School of Law. Reprinted by special permission of Northwestern University School of Law, *The Journal of Criminal Law and Criminology*.

the victim. They often expect—with good reason—that the criminal justice system will share the view that such victims are unworthy of vigorous enforcement of the law. The stereotypes and biases upon which these views are based are, in turn, residues of historical relations of subordination, inequality, and discrimination, which criminals capitalize upon and reinforce. Moreover, like the schoolyard bully who preys upon the small, the weak, and the outcast, crimes against the disadvantaged are increasingly understood to possess a distinct moral status and evoke particular policy implications.

Addressing Hate Crime with Legislation

For students of public policy, advocacy groups, and legislators alike, questions about how law can best respond to the criminal victimization of minorities and others who are systematically disadvantaged presents a pressing, yet familiar, problem. This problem is often stated as a question: should those interested in enhancing the status and welfare of minority groups pursue policies that provide "special" treatment for minorities; or, alternatively, should they pursue policies that ignore the unique social location, special qualities, and socially structured obstacles faced by minorities and work solely towards improving the social and legal resources available to all victims of crime, regardless of their social characteristics or group membership? Stated more succinctly, should all victims of crime be treated the same or should some victims of crime, namely people who face unique barriers when accessing the criminal justice system and pursuing justice, be distinguished and treated differently? Historically and in the current era, policymakers, especially lawmakers, and advocates for minorities have had to respond to this question. And, how they have responded and continue to respond to this question is consequential for the making of criminal law and the delivery of social justice in the United States. . . .

There are costs and benefits associated with both choices to policymaking. Policies that emphasize the "special" needs of minorities, such as affirmative action policies and anti-discrimination laws, can reinforce cultural distinctions between "minorities" and "normals." Such policies can render minorities different from normals, underscore their "incapacities" and special needs as the defining feature of their identities and, ultimately, place them in subordinate positions within both the public and privates spheres of social life. Arguably, one of the unintended consequences of social policies that single out subpopulations for "special" protections and treatment is the reinforcement of the idea that people of color, women, gays and lesbians, the poor, immigrants, those with disabilities, and non-Christians, for example, are more vulnerable members of society, less capable of responding to real and perceived vulnerabilities, and ultimately less credible participants in an array of social activities, especially those interfacing with the criminal justice system.

In contrast, policies that ignore differences between types of victims risk being insensitive to the increasingly well-documented institutional, organizational, and interactional disadvantages faced by minorities, including those who find themselves confronting a criminal justice system with ideologies and structures that were enacted without them in mind. Treating minorities the same as other crime victims does little to challenge the biases and stereotypes with which criminal justice officials often operate. A sizeable body of evidence suggests that ignoring social difference seldom is enough to produce equality, especially in the criminal justice system.

Indeed, as many advocates for people of color, Jews, women, gays, lesbians, and persons with disabilities have recently pointed out, crimes against minorities are often unrecognized or ignored by law enforcement. Failing to acknowledge the differences around which systematic injustices revolve, the argument goes, allows state officials to continue to do business as usual and does little to remedy systematic inequality. . . .

Demand for Hate Crime Laws in the 1980s and 1990s

The *National Law Journal* . . . [in 1994] noted that the 1990s may go down in history as "the decade of hate—or at least of hate crime." Although it remains questionable whether the United States is actually experiencing greater levels of hate-motivated conduct than in the past, it is beyond dispute that the ascendance of the concept of "hate crime" in policy discourse has focused attention on violence motivated by bigotry and manifest as discrimination in a new way. . . . What is now commonly understood as "bias" or "hate" crime is an age-old problem approached with a new conceptual lens and sense of urgency. Despite a well-documented history of violence directed at minorities, during the 1980s and 1990s multiple social movements began to identify and address the problem of discriminatory violence directed at minorities: federal, state, and local governments instituted task forces and commissions to analyze the issue; legislative campaigns sprang up at every level of government; new sentencing rules and categories of criminal behavior were established in law; prosecutors and law enforcement developed special training policies and specialized enforcement units; scholarly commentary and social science research exploded on the topic; and the United States Supreme Court weighed in with its analysis of the laws in three highly controversial cases. As a result of these activities, criminal conduct that was once undistinguished from ordinary crime has been parsed out, redefined, and condemned more harshly than before. And "hate crime" has secured a place in the American political and legal landscape.

These extraordinary developments attest to the growing concern with, visibility of, and public resources directed at violence motivated by bigotry, hatred, or bias. They reflect the increasing acceptance of the idea that criminal conduct is "different" when it involves an act of discrimination. More importantly, for the purposes of this article, it is clear that the law has become the primary institution charged with defining and curbing hate- or bias-motivated violence. Legal reform has been one of—if not the most—dominant response to bias-motivated violence in the United States. During a congressional debate on hate crime [in 1985], Representative Mario Biaggi said it most succinctly when he argued, "the obvious point is that we are dealing with a national problem and we must look to our laws for remedies." Concurring, Representative John Conyers, Jr. explained [in 1998] that the enactment of hate crime legislation "will carry to offenders, to victims, and to society at large an important message, that the Nation is committed to battling the violent manifestations of bigotry." These views reflect a general agreement among state and federal legislators that [as Conyers stated] "hate crimes, which can range from threats and vandalism to arson, assault and murder, are intended not just to harm the victim, but to send a message of intimidation to an entire community of people."

With this solidified view of discriminatory violent conduct in hand, in the 1970s and early 1980s, lawmakers throughout the United States began to respond to what they perceived as an escalation of violence directed at minorities with a novel legal strategy: the criminalization of discriminatory violence, now commonly referred to as "hate crime." As a result, by the turn of the [21st] century, [according to Terry A. Maroney] "in seemingly no time at all, a 'hate crimes jurisprudence' had sprung up."

State Hate Crime Law

[Since 1980] almost every state in the United States has adopted at least one hate crime statute that simultaneously recognizes, defines, and responds to discriminatory violence.

Hate crime statutes have taken many forms throughout the United States, including statutes prescribing criminal penalties for civil rights violations; specific "ethnic intimidation" and "malicious harassment" statutes; and provisions in previously enacted statutes for enhanced penalties if an extant crime is committed for bias or prejudicial reasons. These laws specify provisions for race, religion, color, ethnicity, ancestry, national origin, sexual orientation, gender, age, disability, creed, marital status, political affiliation, involvement in civil or human rights, and armed services personnel. In addition, a few states have adopted statutes that require authorities to collect data on hate- (or bias-) motivated crimes; mandate law enforcement training; prohibit the undertaking of paramilitary training; specify parental liability; and provide for victim compensation. Finally, many states have statutes that prohibit institutional vandalism and the desecration or the defacement of religious objects, the interference with or disturbance of religious worship, cross burning, the wearing of hoods or masks, the formation of secret societies, and the distribution of publications and advertisements designed to harass select groups of individuals. This last group of laws rejects a previous generation of what, in retrospect, could be termed "hate crime" law.

Across the United States, state hate crime laws vary immensely in wording. Some laws employ a language of civil rights. For example, in 1987 California adopted an "Interference with Exercise of Civil Rights" statute that states:

> No person, whether or not acting under the color of law, shall by force or threat of force, willfully injure, intimidate, interfere with, oppress, or threaten any other person in the free exercise or enjoyment of any right or privilege secured to him or her by the constitution or laws of this state or by the Constitution or the laws of the United States because of the other person's race, color, religion, ancestry, national origin, or sexual orientation.

In contrast, some states employ the language of "ethnic intimidation or malicious harassment." In 1983, for example, Idaho adopted a "Malicious Harassment" law that declares:

It shall be unlawful for any person, maliciously and with the specific intent to intimidate or harass another person because of that person's race, color, religion, ancestry, or national origin to: (a) Cause physical injury to another person; or (b) Damage, destroy, or deface any real or personal property of another person; or (c) Threaten, by word or act, to do the acts prohibited if there is reasonable cause to believe that any of the acts described in subsections (a) and (b) of this section will occur. For purposes of this section, "deface" shall include, but not be limited to, cross-burnings, or the placing of any word or symbol commonly associated with racial, religious, or ethnic terrorism on the property of another person without his or her permission.

Finally, some statutes simply increase the penalty for committing an enumerated crime if the defendant committed a criminal act that "evidences" or "demonstrates" prejudice or bigotry based on the victim's real or imagined membership in a legally recognized protected status. For example, in 1989 Montana adopted a "Sentence Enhancement" law that states:

A person who has been found guilty of any offense, except malicious intimidation or harassment, that was committed because of the victim's race, creed, religion, color, national origin, or involvement in civil rights or human rights activities or that involved damage, destruction, or attempted destruction of a building regularly used for religious worship, in addition to the punishment provided for commission of the offense, may be sentenced to a term of imprisonment of not less than 2 years or more than 10 years, except as provided in 46-18-222.

Despite variation in wording, these laws have criminalized select forms of bias-motivated violence.

Federal Hate Crime Legislation

Following the states' lead, the United States Congress has passed three laws specifically designed to address bias-motivated violence and it continues to consider additional legislation. In 1990, President [George H.W.] Bush signed the Hate Crimes Statistics Act, which requires the Attorney General to collect statistical data on "crimes that manifest evidence of prejudice based on race, religion, sexual orientation, or ethnicity, including where appropriate the crimes of murder, non-negligent manslaughter; forcible rape; aggravated assault, simple assault, intimidation; arson; and destruction, damage or vandalism of property." As a data collection law, the Hate Crimes Statistics Act merely requires the Attorney General to gather and make available to the public data on bias-motivated crime, which has been done every year since 1991. It does not, in any way, stipulate new penalties for bias-motivated crimes, nor does it provide legal recourse for victims of bias-motivated crime. The rationale for the Hate Crimes Statistics Act was to mandate the collection of empirical data necessary to develop effective policy. Those supporting it argued that involving the police in identifying and counting hate crimes could help law enforcement officials measure trends, fashion effective responses, design prevention strategies, and develop sensitivity to the particular needs of victims of hate crimes.

In 1994, Congress passed two more hate crime laws. The Violence Against Women Act specifies that "all persons within the United States shall have the right to be free from crimes of violence motivated by gender." The Violence Against Women Act allocated over $1.6 billion for education, rape crisis hotlines, training of justice personnel, victim services (especially shelters for victims of battery), and special units of police and prosecutors to deal with crimes against women. The heart of the legislation, Title III, provides a civil remedy for "gender crimes."

In essence, Title III entitles victims to compensatory and punitive damages through the federal courts for a crime of violence if it is motivated, at least in part, by animus toward the victim's gender. This allowance implicitly acknowledges that some, if not most, violence against women is not gender-neutral; instead, it establishes the possibility that violence motivated by gender animus is a proper subject for civil rights action. In so doing, it defined the term "hate crime" as "a crime of violence committed because of gender or on the basis of gender, and due, at least in part, to animus based on the victim's gender." Although this law was [in 1999] ruled unconstitutional, it was predicated upon and promoted the inclusion of gender in the concept of a hate crime.

Also, in 1994, Congress passed the Hate Crimes Sentencing Enhancement Act. This law identifies eight predicate crimes—murder; nonnegligent manslaughter; forcible rape; aggravated assault; simple assault; intimidation; arson; and destruction, damage, or vandalism of property—for which judges are allowed to enhance penalties of "not less than three offense levels for offenses that the finder of fact at trial determines beyond a reasonable doubt are hate crimes." For the purposes of this law, "hate crime" is defined as criminal conduct wherein "the defendant intentionally selected any victim or property as the object of the offense because of the actual or perceived race, color, religion, national origin, ethnicity, gender, disability, or sexual orientation of any person." Although broad in form, this law addresses only those hate crimes that take place on federal lands and properties.

Finally, the Hate Crimes Prevention Act was introduced in the Senate and House of Representatives. If signed into law, this legislation would

[A]mend the Federal criminal code to set penalties for persons who, whether or not acting under the color of law, willfully cause bodily injury to any person or, through the use of fire, firearm, or explosive device, attempt to cause such injury, because of the actual or perceived: (1) race, color, religion, or national origin of any person; and (2) religion, gender, sexual orientation, or disability of any person, where in connection with the offense, the defendant or the victim travels in interstate or foreign commerce, uses a facility or instrumentality of interstate or foreign commerce, or engages in any activity affecting interstate or foreign commerce, or where the offense is in or affects interstate or foreign commerce.

Although not yet law, this pending legislation broadens the reach of the Hate Crimes Sentencing Enhancement Act. [Editor's note: This legislation is still pending as of 2007.]

The state and federal laws described above show that many contemporary advocates share a commitment to using the law, law enforcement, and the criminal justice system as vehicles to enhance the status and welfare of minority constituencies deemed differentially vulnerable to violence motivated by bigotry. Despite variation in their wording and content, criminal hate crime statutes are laws that criminalize, or further criminalize, activities motivated by bias toward individuals or groups because of their real or imagined characteristics. . . . This definition consists of three elements. First, the law provides a new state policy action, by either creating a new criminal category, altering an existing law, or enhancing penalties for select extant crimes when they are committed for bias reasons. Second, hate crime laws contain an intent standard. In other words, statutes contain wording that refers to the subjective intention of the perpetrator rather than relying solely on the basis of objective behavior. Finally, hate crime laws specify a list of protected social statuses, such as race, religion, ethnicity, sexual orientation, gender, disabilities, etc. These elements of the definition of hate crime law capture the spirit and essence of hate crime legislation designed to punish bias-motivated conduct.

The emergence and proliferation of hate crime law marks an important moment in the history of crime control efforts, the development of criminal and civil law, the allocation of civil rights, and the symbolic status of select minorities in the United States.

The Importance of Hate-Crime Legislation in America

Bill Clinton

During his presidency, Bill Clinton worked to advance hate-crime legislation in America. He convened the first White House Conference on Hate Crimes in 1997 and vocally supported harsher punishments and the Hate Crimes Prevention Act. In the following address to fellow supporters of hate-crime legislation, Clinton portrays hate crime as an issue of the past and of the present, at home and abroad. He emphasizes the importance of being aware of hate-based atrocities around the world and of standing up against them. Clinton served as U.S. president from 1993 to 2001. Since the end of his second term, he has remained active as a speaker and political figure.

Those of us who grew up in the segregated South are perhaps more sensitive to all these various hate crimes issues because we grew up in a culture that was dominated for too long by people who thought they only counted if they had somebody to look down on, that they could only lift themselves up if they were pushing someone else down; that their whole definition of a positive life required a negative definition of another group of people. That's really what this is all about.

And ... if you look at the whole history of this violence we see in Kosovo, what we went through in Bosnia, this, the fifth anniversary of the awful Rwandan genocide, that I regret so much the world was not organized enough to move quickly enough to deal with it before hundreds of thousands of lives were lost—with the oppression of women in Afghanistan,

President Bill Clinton, "Remarks by the President at Hate Crimes Announcement," *White House Education Press Releases and Statements*, April 6, 1999, http://www.ed.gov/PressReleases/04-1999/wh-0406.html.

with the lingering bitterness in the Middle East—you see all these things. When you strip it all away, down deep inside there is this idea that you cannot organize personal life or social life unless some group feels better about itself only when they are oppressing someone else. Or people at least believe that they ought to have the right to do violence against someone else solely because of who they are, not because of what they do. Now, at the bottom, that's what this is all about.

And I have said repeatedly since I have been President that one of the things I have sought to do in our country is to bridge all these divides, and to get all of our people not to agree with one another, not to even like one another all the time—goodness knows, we can't like everybody all the time—but to recognize that our common humanity is more important than these categorical differences. And also to recognize that over the long run, America will not be able to be a force for good abroad unless we are good at home.

If you think about the brave men and women who are working with our NATO [North Atlantic Treaty Organization] allies today in Kosovo, and you remember that this basically all started 12 years ago [in 1987], when Mr. [Slobodan] Milosevic decided to rally the support of his ethnic Serbian group by turning their hatred against the Kosovar Albanians, and later the Bosnian Muslims and the Croatian Catholics, and the others—it is very important that we deal with these challenges here at home, even as we continue to support the work of our people in uniform in the Balkans.

Importance of Awareness of Issues at Home and Abroad

I want to say again, the United States would never choose force as anything other than a last option. And Mr. Milosevic could end it now by withdrawing his military police and paramilitary forces, by accepting the deployment of an international security force to protect not only the Kosovar Albanians, most but not all of whom are Muslims, but also the Serbian minority in Kosovo. Everybody. We're not for anybody's hate crimes. And by making it possible for all the refugees to return and to move toward a political framework based on the accords reached in France.

Now, as I said, we can't continue to organize ourselves to try to stand against these things around the world—which I firmly hope we will. I applaud the women in America who have done so much to bring to the world's attention the terrible treatment of women in Afghanistan, for example. And we have worked hard in Africa to work with other African forces to build an Africa Crisis Response Initiative so that something like the Rwanda genocide cannot happen again. We have to keep working on these things.

But first of all, we must always be working on ourselves. That's really what this is about. Because we know this is more the work of [religious leaders] than the President, but we know that inside each of us there are vulnerabilities to dehumanizing other people simply by putting them in a category that permits us to dismiss them, or that permits us to put them in a category so that on a bad day, when we're feeling especially bad about something we've done, we can say, well, thank God I'm not them. And it is a short step from that—a short, short step from that—to licensing or even participating in acts of violence. . . . It is very easy to get into a social system where you always get to think a little better of yourself because you've always got someone that you can dehumanize.

And that's really what this whole issue with gays is today in America. We're not talking about everybody agreeing with everybody else on every political issue. We're talking about whether people have a right, if they show up and work hard and obey the law, and are good citizens, to pursue their lives and dignity without—free of fear, without fear of being abused.

And this should not be a partisan issue. . . . This ought not to be anything other than a basic, simple statement of American principle.

The Future of Hate May Be Global

But I would like to say one other thing, just as a practical matter. Isn't it interesting to you that we are on the eve of a new century and a new millennium—which will be largely characterized by globalization, the explosion of technology, especially information, and the integration of people—and the number one security threat to that is the persistence of old, even primitive, hatreds? Don't you think that's interesting?

So what I worry about all the time is whether terrorists can get on the Internet and figure out how to make chemical and biological weapons to pursue agendas against people of different ethnic or religious groups. And so it's very humbling, I think, for those of us who think we have brought the modern world, and prosperity and rationality to all of human affairs, to see what is going on in the Balkans, and to see these terrible examples of violence here in our own country. It's very humbling. We should remember that each of us almost wakes up every day with the scales of light and darkness in our own hearts, and we've got to keep them in proper balance. And we have to be, in the United States, absolutely resolute about this.

Hate Crime Is Still a Problem

That's why I think this hate crimes issue is so important. That's why I convened the first White House Conference on Hate Crime. Since then, I would like to say, we have substantially increased the number of FBI agents working on these crimes. We have successfully prosecuted a number of serious cases. We have formed local hate crimes working groups in U.S. Attorneys' offices around the country.

But this is a significant problem. In 1997, . . . over 8,000 hate crime incidents were reported in the United States. That's almost one an hour. Almost one an hour.

So, what are we going to do about it? I would like to mention—we've already talked about the law and I'll say more about that in a minute, but first of all, let me mention three other things. I've asked the Justice Department and the Education Department to include in their annual report card on school safety crucial information on hate crimes among young people both at and away from schools—not only to warn, but to educate.

Secondly, I'm asking the Department of Education to collect important data for the first time on hate crimes and bias on college campuses. Another cruel irony, isn't it—college, the place where we're supposed to have the most freedom, the place where we're supposed to be the most rational, the place where we're supposed to think the highest thoughts with the greatest amount of space. We have significant hate crime problems there, and we need to shine the light on that.

Third, I'm very pleased about this—we are going to have a public-private partnership to help reach middle school students to discuss this whole issue with them and talk about tolerance—why it is a moral, as well as a practical, imperative. And the partnership includes AT&T, Court TV, the National Middle School Association, the Anti-Defamation League, Cable in the Classrooms, as well as the Departments of Education and Justice. I would like to thank them all, because we have to not only punish bad things when they happen, the larger mission is to change the mind, the heart, and the habits of our people when they're young—to keep bad things from happening.

Finally, let me join . . .—in saying, Congress should pass this law [now]. The federal laws already punish some crimes committed against people on the basis of race or religion or national origin, but . . . not all crimes are committed for that purpose. This would strengthen and expand the ability of the Justice Department by removing needless jurisdictional requirements for existing crimes, and giving federal prosecutors the ability to prosecute hate crimes committed because of sexual orientation, gender or disability, along with race and religion.

Now, again I say, when we get exercised about these things—in particular, when someone dies in a horrible incident in America—or when we see slaughter or ethnic cleansing abroad, we should remember that we defeat these things by teaching and by practicing a different way of life, and by reacting vigorously when they occur within our own midst. That is what this is about. And we should remember, whenever we, ourselves, commit even a small slip, where we dehumanize or demonize someone else who is different from us— that every society must teach, practice, and react, if you want to make the most of the world toward which we are moving.

Hate Crimes Prevention Act Is Important

Our diversity is a godsend for us and the world of the 21st century. But it is also the potential for the old, haunting demons that are hard to root out of the human spirit. The Hate Crimes Prevention Act would be important, substantively and symbolically, to send a message to ourselves and to the world that we are going into the 21st century determined to preach and to practice what is right.

Hate-Crime Statistics
Are Misleading

James Lacey

In the ongoing debate about the necessity of hate-crime legislation, both sides draw on statistical information to find out how severe the hate-crime problem really is. Statistics should reveal how many hate-crime victims there are every year, what the crimes committed against them are, what groups are most targeted, what geographical areas are most hit by hate crimes, and who the perpetrators are. This information is invaluable in making philosophical and policy decisions, but how accurate is the information that is gathered in the available statistics? Some argue that statistics are notoriously unreliable and, in the case of hate crimes, easily distorted. With an issue as politically charged as hate-crime law, some experts argue that the statistics should be disregarded if they cannot be trusted.

James Lacey is among those who point to the pitfalls in analyzing hate-crime statistics. He notes that changes in classifications, bias (intentional or not), and the need to guess perpetrators' motives all make statistical information misleading. Worse, he contends, they cover up the basic tolerance and kindness that characterize Americans. Lacey is an Army Reserve colonel who serves as an analyst for the U.S. Joint Forces Command. He draws on his military expertise in his writings about current military events and strategies.

FBI hate-crime data show that crimes against Arabs and Muslims have increased more than 1,500 percent since [2001]. Presumably this seeming outpouring of ethnic hatred is related directly to the aftereffects of Sept. 11. Our shock at

James Lacey, "Hate-Crime Statistics Distort Truth of American Tolerance," *Insight on the News*, vol. 19, no. 2, January 7, 2003, pp. 50–51. Copyright © 2003 News World Communications, Inc. All rights reserved. Reproduced with permission of *Insight*.

that terrible tragedy apparently has created a desire to lash out at innocents who bear a resemblance to the monsters who attacked us.

However, before we drown ourselves in self-recrimination, some perspective is required. It does not take too much peering behind the numbers to show that rather than a nation wracked with hate, we are a people of remarkable forbearance.

Hate-Crime Statistics Are Vulnerable to Bias

Before we look at those numbers though, it needs to be pointed out that hate-crime statistics are politically stacked and arbitrary. They require law-enforcement agencies to look past the crime and determine a person's intent and motivation. It is not enough to say Person A murdered Person B and prosecute accordingly. Now police must determine whether Person B was selected for murder (or any other crime) because he/she was of a different race, ethnicity, religion or sexual orientation than Person A.

Determining what constitutes a hate crime leads to all manner of logical absurdities. For instance: Did a black thief target a white person for robbery because he is white, or did he study the latest socioeconomic data and see that by robbing a white person he is more likely to maximize his potential income? The first would be a hate crime. The second would not.

Because determining a hate crime most often is a judgment call, it allows prejudice and political correctness to enter into the equation. When three white men chained James Byrd to a truck and dragged him to his death, the incident was classified as a hate crime, which it surely was. However, when Colin Ferguson, a black man, boarded a Long Island Railroad train and systematically murdered six whites and wounded 19 others, it was not classified as a hate crime, despite Ferguson's long history of antiwhite outbursts.

In 2001, the FBI recorded 1.7 million acts of interracial violent crime. Of that figure, 1.1 million were cases of blacks committing violent crimes on whites. Despite this, the FBI finds that blacks suffer three times as many hate crimes as whites and as a percentage of the population are almost 30 times more likely to be targeted for a hate crime. Somehow the FBI has peered into the minds of those who committed the 1.1 million acts of black-on-white crime, and determined that there was no racial motivation behind them. That is ridiculous.

Assuming, for now, that law enforcement is equipped with a magical clairvoyance that allows it to look into the hearts of criminals, what then do the numbers tell us?

Classifications Can Skew Conclusions

The 1,500 percent increase in hate crimes against Arabs and Muslims represents 481 actual crimes—up from 28 the year before. Since Arabs previously had been classified as whites, there really is no way to tell if the surge is as great as it appears or if there is just a new sensitivity that allows Arabs to be broken out into a distinct new subset, which no one bothered to do before. In other words, there also may have been 481 hate crimes against Arabs the previous year, but the number was rolled into the larger total and therefore hidden.

Determining What Constitutes a Hate Crime

It also is important to keep in mind what constitutes a hate crime as we consider the "crisis" of hate that Arab-Americans are facing. When people hear the term "hate crime" they almost immediately get an image of the vilest assaults. People may have an image of hate represented by Byrd being dragged behind a truck, but the reality is that most hate crimes are far more prosaic. If a person gets upset at an ethnic Arab and tells him to go back to his own country, for purposes of the record that is as much a hate crime as if he goes out at night looking for Arabs to beat to death.

Still, 481 acts of ethnic hatred are 481 too many. But before the national castigation begins, that number needs to be examined from a new viewpoint. There are more than 3 million Americans of Arab descent (some estimates are as high as 6 million). This means that 0.016 percent of them were victims of a hate crime [in the year under discussion]. This is about the same probability as being hit by lightning in a lifetime. Jews, by comparison, have a 0.019 percent chance of being the victim of a hate crime, which is almost double the chance of a black being the victim.

Whites suffered only 891 hate crimes (0.008 percent) [during that same] year, but as we have seen, that number is suspect. For instance, the whites killed by hate-filled Arab fanatics on Sept. 11 were not classified as victims of a hate crime. Does the fact that the terrorists were targeting Americans in general or that members of other ethnic groups also were killed somehow mitigate the hatred felt toward any particular group?

Americans Are Actually Quite Tolerant

The happy fact is that while there still is hatred in the United States it is dwarfed by the good will and generous spirit of most Americans. In what other country could members of one ethnic group inflict such an incredible blow on a nation and the response be so muted? In the year after Sept. 11, 2001, only a small fraction of a percent of Arabs and Muslims reported being victims of hate. Out of approximately 3 million Arabs in the United States, 2,999,519 of them went about their lives without reporting the slightest bit of harassment. Americans can be justly proud of the tolerance that has been exhibited in the face of so terrible a disaster.

As a side note, the FBI should get out of the mind-reading business. A crime is a crime is a crime, and justice should be applied accordingly. Hate-crime statistics are good only for feeding into the propaganda of race-baiting hatemongers who make their living inflaming racial and ethnic animosity.

First Amendment Issues of Hate Speech and Hate Crimes

Franklyn S. Haiman

Constitutional scholars debate whether hate-crime legislation has constitutional standing, based on First Amendment protection. Supporters of such legislation argue that hate speech is so closely tied to hate crimes that it reveals the criminal's state of mind when committing the crime. Further, hate speech—verbal or written—is invaluable in determining that a crime committed was indeed a hate crime. In the following viewpoint, Franklyn S. Haiman helps readers understand the First Amendment issues that are relevant to the hate-crime debate. His position is that hate-crime legislation is necessary and that such laws have strong constitutional standing.

Haiman is the John Evans Professor Emeritus of Communication Studies at Northwestern University. He is the author of books and articles on free speech and communication ethics, including Speech and Law in a Free Society. *The National Communication Association honored Haiman by creating the Franklyn Haiman Award for Distinguished Scholarship in Freedom of Speech.*

There are two reasons for considering the possibility that the First Amendment may be implicated in criminal convictions for [hate crimes]. The first is that one purpose of the criminal act, if not the primary purpose, may be to send a political or social message to the world, such as a warning that African Americans are not welcome in a particular neighborhood, or that gay men had better go back into the closet or else risk physical harm. The second reason is that the only

Franklyn S. Haiman, *"Speech Acts" and the First Amendment.* Carbondale: Southern Illinois University Press, 1993, pp. 35–48. Copyright © 1993 by the Board of Trustees, Southern Illinois University. All rights reserved. Reproduced by permission of the publisher.

way to identify group hatred as the motivation is by statements the perpetrator has made or by other symbolic behavior engaged in before, during, or after the commission of the crime.

Neither of these reasons justifies calling the crimes speech acts, any more than a bank robbery becomes a speech act because one of the gunmen speaks to the tellers and orders them to "stick 'em up." These are physical behaviors with speech ingredients, just the converse of an oration, which is speech behavior with the physical ingredient of noise. But whereas the noise made by a speech does not usually cause us to believe that the speech should be suppressed, the speech involved in a hate crime *may* cause us to think that penalties greater than what would normally apply to such a crime are justified. . . .

Free Speech Concerns

The first question I raised above is whether the act should be entitled to First Amendment protection if it has been committed for the sole or primary purpose of sending a message to the world, with the immediate target being perhaps an incidental or random victim. This claim cannot be taken seriously. Trespass, defacement or destruction of property, assault and battery, arson, and murder are made criminal by the law because of the substantial physical harm they do to their victims. Those harms occur regardless of any possible communicative purposes the perpetrator may have had in mind, and those purposes cannot be accepted as an excuse for the behavior if a safe and peaceful society is to be maintained.

Where the offense in question is arguably a victimless crime with no palpable injury to others, and the purpose is to communicate a message, one cannot be so cavalier in dismissing a free speech claim. But that is true whether the alleged offender seeks First Amendment protection against an *en-*

hanced penalty for a bias-motivated act or against *any* penalty for any behavior that would normally be punishable. . . .

The second free speech concern about enhanced penalties for hate crimes is indeed a serious one, for the only way one can know that a hate crime has been committed is if the perpetrators have revealed their motivation by expressing it verbally or symbolically. If a gang of hoodlums jumps out of a car and beats up a gay man on the sidewalk, at the same time yelling, "You lousy queer," or if swastikas are painted on a temple wall, we know that a hate crime has been committed. But if those same hoodlums beat up a gay man and say nothing and give no evidence in their previous statements that they were looking for gay men to beat up, or if graffiti with no clear meaning is scrawled on a temple wall, we have no way of knowing or proving a group hatred motivation. Thus, it might fairly be claimed, and has been claimed, that to impose heavier penalties on those who have expressed racist views than on those who have kept their views to themselves is to punish the former for their beliefs and their speech, in violation of the First Amendment.

A state court judge in Michigan made this argument in strong language when he found that state's ethnic intimidation law to be unconstitutional. The case involved a defendant charged with both arson and ethnic intimidation in the burning of the home of an African American family. While letting the arson charge stand, the judge dismissed the ethnic intimidation charge on the grounds that the state statute was both vague and violative of the First Amendment:

> It is claimed that the statute punishes conduct rather than words or expression. This argument has a hollow ring, as the punishable conduct, namely physical contact or damaging, destroying, or defacing real or personal property, is already punishable under other criminal statutes. What is punished is the spoken or written word or expression thereof by conduct. There are numerous instances where this statute

can be applied to convert conduct, which would normally be a misdeameanor, into a felony merely because of the spoken word. For example, A strikes B in the face with his fists thereby committing a misdemeanor commonly known as assault and battery. However, should A add just one word, such as "kraut," "wop," "frog," "honkie," "nigger," "bitch," "Hebrew," "queer," it becomes a felony; and A will be punished not for his conduct alone, a misdemeanor, but for using the spoken word. [*People v. Justice*, Michigan District Court, 1990]

It is of additional interest that in this case the evidence that the crime was motivated by group hatred came not from any statements directed at the victims or from any utterances made to others before or during the commission of the act, but from remarks the defendant made to friends after the fact, when he was apparently drunk.

Enhanced Penalties Justifiable

There is no getting around the argument that enhanced penalties for hate crimes do, indeed, punish people, in part, for the verbal or symbolic expression of their beliefs and attitudes. But whether that should automatically be considered a violation of their First Amendment rights, as the Michigan judge and others have concluded, is a very different matter. To begin with, they are, or should be, punished only when their beliefs and attitudes have resulted in the commission of a crime. Moreover, those beliefs and attitudes are the basis only for judging the severity of their crime and the appropriate degree of punishment, not for deciding whether they will be punished at all. Enhanced penalties for hate crimes are arguably comparable to the differences in punishment among first-degree murder, second-degree murder, and manslaughter, where the victim is just as dead, but the motivation or state of mind of the killer determines the gravity of the crime and the punishment. If the killing occurred in self-defense, which is another state of mind, it does not even constitute a crime, for the *mens rea* (bad mind) required by the law is missing. Although there are serious hazards to the fair administration of justice any time a court probes into the state of mind of those charged with criminal acts, and particularly when dealing with attitudes like group hatred, it is a necessary enterprise if one accepts the premise, as I do, that bias-motivated crimes pose a greater danger to the peace and safety of society than equivalent crimes that are not so motivated. . . .

Concerns About Discrimination

I . . . have concerns about the discriminatory enforcement that may occur when hate crime laws are on the books, but . . . I do not see a unique problem, for instance, with the police invoking such laws more readily against the members of disadvantaged, than advantaged, groups. Such discrimination is a serious but generic problem of *all* law enforcement and needs to be addressed at that broader level, not solely with respect to the enforcement of hate crime laws. I am also not . . . troubled . . . by the possibility that "well-meaning officers and prosecutors" may add a charge of ethnic intimidation any time a crime is committed by a person of one ethnicity against a victim of another group. If the law enforcement officials are really well-meaning, that is not likely to happen unless they have some reason to believe that group hatred was the stimulus for the crime.

What does concern me a great deal is a [another] kind of discriminatory enforcement. . . . It is the fact that only those offenders who are outspoken about their group biases and hatreds will be subjected to enhanced penalties for their crimes, whereas those who may have had exactly the same motivation, but kept their beliefs and attitudes to themselves, will escape the added punishment. This concern is somewhat alleviated by my assumption that most group haters who commit criminal acts are not likely to be secretive about their attitudes and motivations. For one thing, it would be very difficult for them never to have revealed those attitudes and motivations to other people who might become potential witnesses against them. On the contrary, they are more likely to be proud of their views and actions and to want them to be known, at least in circles they presume to be sympathetic.

But perhaps more important is the fact that if the purpose of their crime is to send a political or social message to the world, that message may not get across unless they accompany their action with words or symbols that reveal its motivation. If they beat up a gay man and say nothing, paint meaningless graffiti on a temple wall, or set fire to the home of an African American family without simultaneously communicating some kind of verbal warning to other African Americans, their criminal act may speak for itself, but that would require a particular inference being made by the public, an inference that may not have been clearly indicated. If offenders want to be sure to get their message across, they are more likely to make it verbally or symbolically explicit.

Having said all this, I still recognize the problem that those who speak out most clearly about their hatreds will be the ones subjected to enhanced penalties, and those who are smart enough, or devious enough, to successfully hide their motivations will not be. It reminds me of the situation a number of years ago after Congress enacted the requirement that all young men register for the draft on reaching their eighteenth birthday. Apparently, several thousand men, out of conscience or negligence, did not comply with this requirement, but only a relatively small number of them—primarily those who had spoken out publicly against the law—were prosecuted by the government. The argument was made in their defense that this selective pattern of law enforcement was a violation of the First Amendment because punishment was being meted out only to those who had exercised their freedom of speech. Whether it should have or not, that argument failed to win judicial agreement. The men who were prosecuted were, after all, in clear violation of the law, and the fact that other violators were not also pursued was viewed as entirely within the discretion of prosecuting officials, just as prosecutions for all offenses are ultimately left to the discretion of law enforcement officers.

Conclusion

I return now to the large question posed at the outset of this [viewpoint]. Are there countervailing free speech interests that should cause us to refrain from combating the dangers that hate crimes pose to society by imposing enhanced penalties on such behavior? Those dangers should not be minimized. In addition to the injury they inflict on their immediate targets, hate crimes exacerbate already hazardous racial and ethnic tensions, and may engender fear in members of victim groups to the point that they hesitate to walk on the sidewalks of their own community or venture into the territory of others to work, to live, or to engage in their other normal pursuits. In weighing those harms against the relatively minimal intrusions into the First Amendment arena that a carefully drafted enhanced penalty law may entail, I come hesitantly to the conclusion that such laws are constitutionally acceptable. As to whether they are wise as a matter of public policy, I am quite unsure and thus leave that question for others to answer.

Hate Crimes Deserve Harsher Punishments

Howard P. Berkowitz

The controversy surrounding whether hate crimes warrant special status and harsher punishments in the criminal justice system is far from settled. Supporters of such legislation, such as Howard P. Berkowitz, argue that perpetrators of hate crimes are inherently deserving of harsher penalties because they attack entire communities when they attack their hand-picked victims. As a result, hate crimes are particularly divisive and harmful to society as a whole. People feel safer, Berkowitz maintains, from random acts of violence than from crimes that would single them out for personal vendettas.

Berkowitz is a past national chairman of the Anti-Defamation League, a nonprofit organization established to combat bigotry through education and political activism. He is currently the president of the Washington Institute for Near East Policy, a think tank on foreign policy.

Hate crimes, whether directed against one person or many, are particularly destructive in the way they spread feelings of hurt, anxiety and fear. A hate crime is more than an attack on an individual. It is an assault on an entire community. And for this reason alone it is important to send a message that criminals who commit bias crimes will pay the price.

Critics of hate-crimes legislation have used colorful prose to dismiss the laws as "identity politics" and "theatrical empathy," arguing the statutes are a strong-handed attempt to impose a politically correct ideology and an affront to basic constitutional rights.

Howard P. Berkowitz, "Symposium," *Insight on the News*, vol. 15, no. 35, September 20, 1999, p. 40. Copyright © 1999 News World Communications, Inc. All rights reserved. Reproduced with permission of *Insight*.

Hate Crimes Are Frequent and Brutal

However, there has been no shortage of horrifying assaults on blacks, Jews and other minorities, which would seem to call this oversimplified view into question. Crimes predicated on race and ethnicity are becoming more and more virulent in this country. They are being committed by individuals with links to organized hate groups operating on the farthest fringes of American society—groups whose outreach is widening due to advances in technology, most notably the Internet.

The crimes have been shocking in their brutality. A man who, according to police, was bent on issuing a "wake-up call to America to kill Jews" builds up an arsenal capable of wreaking vast amounts of bloodshed and barges—guns blazing—into a Jewish community center. Before his bloody rampage was over, Buford O. Furrow Jr. had shot and wounded 5- and 6-year-olds, a teen-ager and a woman before taking the life of a Filipino-American postal worker whom Furrow identified as a "target of opportunity" because of his race.

Weeks earlier, Benjamin Nathaniel Smith, an avowed racist with ties to the virulently anti-Semitic and racist World Church of the Creator, had gone on a killing rampage through the Midwest. The targets again were minorities—Orthodox Jews on their way home from synagogue, blacks and Asian-Americans. The carnage resulted in the deaths of former basketball coach Ricky Byrdsong and a Korean-American graduate student, slain as he emerged from church in Bloomington, Ind.

Smith's targets also were chosen carefully and, like the three synagogues in Sacramento, Calif., which were damaged by arson in July [1999], his crimes affected people engaged in, or on their way to, worship. Near one of the synagogues in Sacramento, police found hate literature and later discovered evidence possibly linking two brothers arrested in connection with another hate crime—the brutal slaying of a homosexual couple—to the synagogue fires.

Hate Crime Legislation Sends a Strong Message

All of this hate activity has left us, as Americans, grappling for answers. Everyone agrees that something, legislative or otherwise, must be done to stem the tide of hate. The Anti-Defamation League, or ADL, as a leader in the fight against anti-Semitism, hatred and bigotry, believes strong hate-crimes legislation is one answer. We do not view penalty enhancement as a panacea, a cure-all for the scourge of hate in society. But it is important—a rational, fair-minded message to bigots and racists everywhere—that society will not tolerate crimes that single out an individual because of his or her race, religion, national origin or color. Penalty-enhancement statutes put criminals on notice that the consequences for committing hate crimes are severe.

Aside from sensational crimes, government statistics also make a compelling argument for the necessity of strong hate-crimes statutes. Since 1991 the FBI has documented more than 50,000 hate crimes. In 1996 alone, 8,759 hate crimes were reported in the United States. In 1997, . . . the number rose to 9,861—the highest number of hate crimes ever recorded by the FBI in a single year. Still many more hate crimes go undocumented. The numbers continue to rise as the casualties mount.

Hate Crimes Are Uniquely Unsettling

Legislators across the country, state and federal, recognize the special trauma hate crimes cause, the sense of vulnerability and fear they foster and the polarizing effect they can have on entire communities. Lawmakers understand their responsibility to provide criminal sanctions that reflect our collective societal judgment regarding the relative seriousness of criminal offenses.

While all crimes are upsetting, a hate crime is particularly disturbing because of the unique impact not only on the victim but also on the victim's community. Bias crimes are designed to intimidate, leaving people feeling isolated, vulnerable and unprotected. Failure to address this unique type of crime can cause an isolated incident to explode into widespread community tension. The damage cannot be measured solely in terms of physical injury or dollars and cents. By making minority communities fearful, angry and suspicious of other groups—and of the legal structure that is supposed to protect them—these incidents can damage the fabric of our society and fragment communities.

Hate-Crime Laws Do Not Violate the First Amendment

Opponents of hate-crimes legislation often will argue that the laws represent the worst aspects of Orwellian thought control and intrude on the sanctity of the First Amendment. These critics erroneously contend that such statutes punish individuals for their beliefs and their speech. In making this flawed argument, the critics demonstrate a fundamental misunderstanding of hate-crimes legislation as well as the First Amendment.

The fact is hate-crimes legislation does not in any way target or punish speech; such statutes punish conduct only. Individuals remain free to express any view about race, religion, sexuality or any other topic. It is only when they act on their prejudices or callously select their victims based on personal characteristics such as race or religion that hate-crimes statutes come into play. Such legislation simply says that someone who attacks a black or a Jew because he is black or Jewish will receive an enhanced penalty. Such an approach by no means is new to criminal law. Legislators, law-enforcement officials and judicial officers frequently consider motive—in charges ranging from the mundane, such as burglary, to the exceptional, such as treason—to determine whether a crime, or what class of crime, has been committed.

The U.S. Supreme Court has supported that view. In 1993, in a landmark 9-0 decision, the court upheld a Wisconsin penalty-enhancement statute, ruling that the state was right in seeking to increase the sentence for an African-American man who had encouraged and participated in an attack on a young white man. In *Wisconsin vs. Mitchell*, the high court ruled that the statute aimed to discourage conduct that is not protected by the First Amendment and that the state had a special interest in punishing bias crimes. The court's decision removed any doubt that legislatures properly may increase the penalties for criminal activity in which the victim is targeted because of his race, religion, sexual orientation, gender, ethnicity or disability.

Criteria of Hate-Crimes Legislation

Hate-crimes legislation is important because it is a message from society and the legislature that bias crimes will not be tolerated. To date [1999], 40 states and the District of Columbia have enacted hate-crimes statutes, as has the federal government. The most effective kind of hate-crimes law, often based on model legislation introduced by the ADL, provides for enhanced penalties when a perpetrator chooses his victim based on race, religion or another protected category. When prejudice prompts an individual to engage in criminal conduct, a prosecutor may seek a more severe sentence but must prove, beyond a reasonable doubt, that the victim intentionally was selected because of personal characteristics. The intent of penalty-enhancement hate-crimes laws is not only to reassure targeted groups by imposing serious punishment on hate-crime perpetrators but also to deter these crimes by demonstrating that they will be dealt with seriously and swiftly.

Constitutional and effective penalty-enhancement statutes must continue to be enacted at the federal and state levels. According to the current federal law—18 U.S.C. Sec. 245—before the federal government can prosecute a hate crime, it must prove both that the crime occurred because of a person's membership in a designated group and because (not simply while) the victim was engaged in certain specified federally protected activities, such as serving on a jury, voting or attending public schools. Thus, while federal law protects Americans from hate crimes in voting booths and schools, it does not protect them from similar crimes in their homes or on the streets. Presently, it is left to the discretion of the local officials whether to prosecute the crime as a hate crime. . . .

Laws Necessary in Today's Society

In these increasingly violent times, hate-crimes legislation is a strong and necessary response to combat criminal acts of prejudice and bias. Current hate-crimes laws are both valuable and constitutional. They only punish acts of violence; they neither condemn private beliefs nor chill constitutionally protected speech. The statutes guarantee that perpetrators of bias crimes will be punished in proportion to the seriousness of the crimes they have committed. The laws protect all Americans, allowing them to walk the streets safe in the knowledge that their community will not tolerate violent bigotry.

Hate Crimes Do Not Deserve Harsher Punishments

James Q. Wilson

While most people agree that hate crimes are despicable, not everyone agrees that they should have a separate status among crimes. Opponents of hate-crime legislation, such as James Q. Wilson, maintain that a crime motivated by hate is no more tragic or horrifying than one motivated by greed, lust, revenge, peer pressure, drunkenness, or any other motive. Wilson adds that giving hate crimes special status and assigning them harsher penalties panders to political correctness, which should not dictate criminal justice. Instead, he argues, the judicial system should impose stricter penalties for all crimes, thereby protecting everyone who has been victimized.

Wilson has been on the faculties of Harvard and UCLA and currently holds the position of Ronald Reagan Professor of Public Policy at Pepperdine University. He has authored numerous articles and books on crime, human nature, and morality. He is the recipient of the Presidential Medal of Freedom. He has also been awarded the American Political Science Association's James Madison Award, as well as a Lifetime Achievement Award.

National tragedies sometimes give rise to comic responses. When Buford Furrow killed a letter carrier and shot several children in Los Angeles, these despicable acts by a neo-Nazi stimulated a national desire to make sure "something was done" to prevent such disasters. One response was to call for tougher gun-control measures, though Furrow had already broken the law when he acquired the weapons he used. Some new gun-control laws may in fact be needed, but the most important thing is to enforce the ones we already have.

James Q. Wilson, "Hate and Punishment," *National Review*, vol. 51, no. 8, September 13, 1999, p. 18. Copyright © 1999 by National Review, Inc., 215 Lexington Avenue, New York, NY 10016. Reproduced by permission.

Intent Is Important, Not Motive

The other reaction was to call for the passage of tougher laws against "hate crimes." The reason for this demand was that it is important to punish the motive for the crime as well as the crime itself.

Which is an odd view. Suppose there were three men named Furrow, each of whom killed from a different motive. Alfred Furrow shot a letter carrier because he had taken out a life-insurance policy on him and wanted to collect the benefits. Buford Furrow shot one because he disliked people of different ethnic backgrounds. Charles Furrow shot one because he wanted to prove to fellow gang members that he was a tough guy.

Legally, these crimes are identical. That is, they all constitute premeditated murder. Each Furrow not only intended to take a life, he thought through the murder in advance. To prove this in court, a prosecutor must show, usually from inferences based on the defendant's conduct, that the killer deliberated about his actions and acted in accord with those deliberations. The intent of each Furrow was the same.

To convict someone, showing intent—but not motive—is essential. A motive is ordinarily not important in any criminal conviction. The reason is that intent differs from motive. The former has to do with the desire to kill someone, the latter with what state of affairs the killing is supposed to achieve. It usually makes no difference whether an intentional killing was motivated by a desire to get rich, to kill immigrants, or to prove one's toughness. They are all premeditated murder. There is no reason, absent some differences in their backgrounds, why the three Furrows should be punished differently.

There are, to be sure, cases where motive may make a difference. If the evidence of the crime is entirely circumstantial, showing that the suspect had a motive may help establish guilt. And there are certain kinds of murder—for example, killing a police officer or killing in the course of treason—where motive can escalate the penalty. But in these cases the motive can be shown by objective evidence, not by speculating about subjective states.

Hate-crime laws are an effort to make the subjective motive matter. But why should it? Why should hating immigrants be a worse motive than stealing money or earning entree into a criminal gang? The proposed Hate Crimes Prevention Act of 1999 [still pending as of 2007] tries to answer that question by saying that "Congress finds" that hate-motivated violence "disrupts the tranquillity and safety of communities and is deeply divisive" and that it is "a relic of slavery." Congress, of course, has no evidence that either of these statements is true. If people killed others in order to gain money or strengthen gangs, as in fact they do, this would affect the safety of communities and would be deeply divisive at least as much as, and probably more than, killing others because of what they look like. And since the hate-crimes bill would impose tougher penalties on murderers who attack people because of their religion, national origin, gender, or disability, as well as their race or color, it cannot be that the law intends to correct the defects of slavery.

Sentencing Issues

The bill would impose on people convicted of causing bodily injury—not death, just bodily injury—a sentence of up to ten years in prison. Compare that maximum penalty with the penalty people now pay for aggravated assault, which is less than four years in prison. And that penalty could fall on people who break state laws as well, not only federal ones, because hate crosses state boundaries.

This bill would be on top of the hate-crimes provision embedded in current federal sentencing guidelines. This existing provision is even more sweeping than the proposed bill (though, unlike the bill, it applies only to federal defendants).

A person convicted in federal court of having intentionally selected victims because of their "race, color, religion, national origin, ethnicity, gender, disability, or sexual orientation" would have his penalty escalated by moving his crime up three levels on the federal guidelines.

These sentencing rules are baffling. If a man rapes a woman, that is an abomination. Should it make a difference that he chose the rape victim because she was a woman? (Who else would he choose?) Or should it make a difference that the rape resulted from hating women more than from sexual lust? If a gay man rapes another man—another abomination—does it make a difference that a gay man prefers another man as his sexual partner? Or that the victim was raped because he was a man rather than because it gave the rapist sexual pleasure?

Hate Is No Worse a Motive than Any Other

In his splendid novel *Brain Storm*, Richard Dooling describes the case of a fictional man who murders a deaf African American. If he chose the victim because he was deaf or black, he faces a tougher penalty than if he chose him because his wife had an adulterous affair with the victim or because he wanted money the victim had. The novel explores the utter silliness of this legal theory. In an appeals-court hearing, one judge asks the prosecutor whether there is any reason that the hate-crimes law should not also bar selecting victims because of their views on the draft, global warming, or reproductive rights.

And this is hardly a ludicrous extension of an otherwise sound idea. The California hate-crimes law adds to the customary ethnic and sexual categories two more grounds for extra punishment: the victim's "political affiliation" and "position in a labor dispute." If you beat up a person because he was walking a picket line in front of your factory, you get an additional one to three years in prison. If you beat him up only because he had an affair with your wife, you escape these extra penalties. If you are convicted on "hate" grounds and manage to receive probation, you must agree to complete a course on "racial or ethnic sensitivity." The therapeutic state has truly arrived.

All Crime Injures Society, Not Just Hate Crime

California authorities reason that it is important to impose these special penalties because violent crimes aimed at members of a specified group inflict greater injury on society than does "randomly inflicted violent crime." Really? All of these years I had let myself be persuaded that what actually frightened Americans was our high murder rate, almost all of which is anything but random in the sense that it is chiefly aimed at lovers, rival drug dealers, drunken enemies, and the like. The California deep thinkers imagine that having 20,000 homicides a year in America is less important than the unknown, but quite small and almost surely declining, number of hate murders.

Of course, the idea of hate crimes might be given some meaning if we added to the list of protected categories the reasons for actual murders. From now on, let us suppose you will get an extra penalty if you select your victims because they are lovers, rival drug dealers, or drunken enemies. But don't stop here. Let's add to that list victims who belong to a hostile Mafia gang or a rival terrorist faction. And don't forget the Oklahoma City bombing: We should give special protection to government employees and their visitors. Oh, and the bombing of Pan Am Flight 103: more protection for people targeted because they travel by air.

Tougher Existing Penalties to Protect Everyone

There are only two ways to think about violence: Either we penalize all violence more than we now do (which is my view) or we convert the homicide and assault statutes into some combination of affirmative-action quotas and Americans with Disabilities Act benefits. Can you think of any group that does not deserve special protection? If not, every group should be covered by the law—which is just another way of saying that the existing criminal penalties are too weak.

But of course the authors of the hate-crime laws—Rep. John Conyers and Sen. Ted Kennedy, in the case of the present proposal—are not interested in making the laws against violent crimes tougher. They are interested in giving special protection to a few groups. They are interested, in short, in making the criminal law an affirmative-action schedule. They want the law to be tough on people who kill blacks, immigrants, Jews, or gays and lesbians, all of whom, to be sure, have been the object of some degree of social oppression. And they want to give some additional protection to women. Thus, when the proposed law speaks of protecting people selected on the basis of "gender," the authors do not want to protect Caucasian males. I find it hard to believe that federal prosecutors, equipped with this law, will go around looking for white males who have been beaten up by black gangs.

Better Solutions for Addressing Hate Crime

But giving protection to groups that have suffered from abuse is possible within the existing criminal law without adding to the definition of a crime some vague notion of ethnic or sexual motive. The first way is to allow judges to take into account the entire circumstances of the crime—including the motives of the offenders—in determining a penalty. We do this now for almost every offender. That is the place where motives ordinarily enter into the criminal law. But the judges must have discretion in this matter. They cannot be told in advance that hurting a member of one group is more important than hurting a member of a different one, or even that the victim's identity is more important than the criminal's background.

159

The second way is to encourage the FBI, and equivalent state agencies, to put organized hate groups under greater surveillance. Arguments have been made of late that the Justice Department unduly restrains such surveillance. In all likelihood, such restraints arose when the department had to clamp down on the FBI's COINTELPRO program aimed at far-left and Marxist organizations in the 1960s. But it is possible that the restraints have gone too far. At one time, the Ku Klux Klan, however numerous its members, became an ineffectual organization because so many of its members were FBI informants. The same strategy should be aimed at far-right organizations that endorse views that, if acted on, would impose a threat to innocent people.

Hate-Crime Laws Ultimately Ineffective

However questionable—in some cases, ludicrous—the content of hate-crime laws, they are not likely to have much effect. For one thing, such crimes are not that common, at least in the sense that a premeditated murder or assault reflects an ethnic or sexual bias. Those cases in which that kind of premeditation existed have been given great publicity of late. But the very fact of their publicity speaks to their rarity. If such crimes occurred every day, the press would not give them special attention. Of course, ethnic or sexual hostility may well exist in many assaults, but not out of premeditation. Two men get into a fight. They have been drinking and they quarrel about a woman or a football team. Very quickly their ethnicity may become a factor in their argument and in the justification they later make to friends about why they kicked the stuffing out of the other guy. But such offenses lack the degree of prior intent to make them subject to hate-crime laws.

Prosecutors will take advantage of hate-crime provisions to make a name for themselves in high-profile cases. Defense attorneys will recruit psychologists (and, if necessary, witch doctors) to "prove" that there was no real hate and to recruit jurors who believe that it is all right for a member of one ethnic group to beat up a member of a different one. And so we will have high-profile "hate" cases that will draw our attention and lead, no doubt, to more political demands for even tougher laws—on these crimes, but not others.

Suppose Buford Furrow had been kept in jail instead of put on probation. He would not have had a chance, at least for a few years, to shoot at innocent Jewish children. Making the likelihood of punishment greater is more important than stigmatizing the motive of the offender.

Hate-Crime Laws Are Effective and Necessary

Patrick Jordan

Hate crimes are unique among crimes for their motives and the frequent lack of remorse felt by the attackers. There is a huge body of literature supporting the need for legislation that addresses hate crimes specifically and uniquely. Those who support hate-crime legislation point to the uniqueness of hate crimes and the inherent powerlessness of most of their victims. These supporters contend that for many targets of hate crimes—gays, lesbians, ethnic minorities, the disabled, and others—there may be no other path to justice than the law. Writers like Patrick Jordan in the following viewpoint seek to rally support for hate-crime legislation for these very reasons. Jordan offers a basic overview of why hate crime legislation is both effective and necessary. Jordan is managing editor of Commonweal, *where he writes extensively on current events and hotly debated issues of the day.*

The brutal murder of Matthew Shepard—the twenty-one-year-old gay college student in Wyoming who was beaten and tied to a cross-like fence to die—struck at the conscience of the nation. It was not only the sheer sadism and rancor of the crime that affected Americans, but the sense that Shepard's rights had been violated simply for being who he was.

Hate Crimes Are by Nature Unique

Hate-motivated crimes have their own pedigree, their own smell. They are acts of criminal violence—among them kidnapping, torture, and murder—but their destructive capacity stems from a motivational intensity that sets them apart.

Patrick Jordan, "Call Haters to Account: A Case for Bias-Crime Laws," *Commonweal*, vol. 125, no. 20, November 20, 1998, pp. 6–7. Copyright © 1998 Commonweal Publishing Co., Inc. Reproduced by permission of Commonweal Foundation.

When James Byrd, Jr., a disabled African-American, was dragged to his death in Jasper, Texas, every reflective American knew instinctively that this crime was motivated by a particular loathing born of prejudice.

Crimes of this sort can be triggered by a victim's demeanor, color, status, ethnicity, speech, etc., which become the pretext for unleashing blind fury. For potential victims, they threaten the solidarity that binds society together; they undermine the very notion of equality.

Policy Considerations

Twenty-one states have laws that increase the penalties for hate crimes related to race, religion, color, national origin, and sexual orientation. A further nineteen have laws that cover most of the above, but not sexual orientation, even though the FBI reports that 12 percent of hate crimes in 1996 had to do with sexual orientation, and the Southern Poverty Law Center calculates that bias attacks against gays and lesbians are more than twice as likely as similarly motivated attacks on African-Americans, more than six times as likely as those directed at Jews and Hispanics. Ten states, Wyoming among them, have no such laws, and thoughtful people argue they are not needed. In Wyoming, after all, the death penalty is in force for murder, and criminals should be punished for their deeds, not their beliefs.

But whereas the rate of violent crime in general has been falling nationally, violence against gays, lesbians, and transsexuals has been on the rise. [In 1997] in New York City, for example, violent crime fell 10 percent while antigay violence rose by 14 percent, according to the National Coalition of Antiviolence Programs (NCAVP), a gay advocacy group. When a Wyoming legislator likens homosexuals to gay bulls—worthless except to be sent off to the packing plant—the likelihood of a decline in bias crimes is not improved.

Those who question the legality and wisdom of hate-crime legislation, such as columnist George Will, contend that present statutes are sufficient to prosecute hate-motivated crimes, and that to codify "an ever more elaborate structure of identity politics" will not only prove costly but will enhance divisiveness. Others argue that such statutes diminish the constitutional protection against double jeopardy for the same crime. Still another caveat is that such legislation might limit individuals' free speech. In fact, Matthew Shepard's father, Dennis Shepard, warned after his son's death that legislators should not rush to pass "all kinds of new hate-crime laws. Be sure," he said, "you're not taking away any rights of others. . . ."

Yet, as Will grants, "law has the expressive function of stigmatizing particular conduct." Bias-crime laws are less about punishment than about deterrence. Law sends a powerful and effective message that society will not tolerate certain acts. Brian Levin of Stockton College's Center on Hate and Extremism notes that a Boston statute cut hate crimes by two-thirds. A further consideration concerns local and state officials who fail to assure citizens' rights. When there is an absence of federal oversight, victims may lack adequate recourse. Proponents of the proposed Hate-Crimes Prevention Act of 1998 (S. 1529) argue that while many local jurisdictions have attempted to respond to hate-motivated violence, the problem is sufficiently serious and widespread to warrant federal intervention. To shield citizens from the double-jeopardy conundrum, S. 1529 specifically excluded "duplicate punishment for substantially the same offense."

Hate Crimes Are Personal

There are other reasons to support federal involvement besides the fact that homosexuals suffer higher rates of violent hate crime than any other group. One is that violence against gays is more often directed at their persons than at their property. Whereas the Anti-Defamation League reports that 55 percent of anti-Jewish incidents are against persons, the NCAVP offers evidence that 95 percent of violence against gays is directed at their persons.

Another reason to support such legislation is the matter of who will protect victims when local enforcement agencies are themselves biased. In 1997, only 24 percent of antigay incidents tracked nationally by the NCAVP were reported to the police (half the percentage-rate for reporting violent crime in general) because gays feared going to the authorities. Of those gays who did try to file, 12 percent stated that the local police refused to register their complaints; and of those who actually managed to file, almost half said they had been treated indifferently or with hostility. Worse, according to the NCAVP, incidents of antigay abuse by the police themselves jumped nationally from 266 in 1996 to 468 [in 1997].

The American Jewish Committee (AJC)—no stranger to combating crimes of hate—has noted that proposed federal legislation would continue to leave responsibility for protecting citizens' rights primarily with state and local agencies; and that federal prosecution in hate-crime cases has been used only sparingly in the past (6 percent of incidents). Yet the cumulative effect of such federal laws, the AJC points out, has enhanced deterrence, particularly in states that lack laws or do not enforce them.

The murder of Matthew Shepard was not the first and will not be the last crime of its kind. But it should shake our indifference and lead to actions that reduce such crimes. While legislation itself will not change all hearts, it might send a powerful message to some hate-twisted minds.

Hate-Crime Laws Are Ineffective as Deterrents

Richard Kim

An important issue in the debate on hate-crime legislation is the effectiveness of such laws in the real world. Just because laws are passed does not mean that they will have the intended effect, according to Richard Kim in the following viewpoint. Kim argues that not only will laws do nothing to change people's minds and deter them from committing hate-based crimes against innocent people, but police are unlikely to take such laws seriously. Kim argues that law enforcement is itself guilty of mistreating people based on race, sexual orientation, or socioeconomic status. Expecting the same officers to become sympathetic and protective is naïve. While measures should be taken against hate crimes, there are better places to concentrate efforts.

Kim is a frequent contributor to the Nation, Salon, *and the* San Francisco Chronicle, *where he writes about controversial current issues, especially gay and lesbian issues. He also teaches American studies at Skidmore College in upstate New York.*

For whatever reasons, it took the death of a young gay white man at the hands of two other young white men in Wyoming to bring the issue of violence aimed at lesbians, gays, bisexuals and transgendered people (LGBT) to national consciousness. While one of those young men, Russell Henderson, has pleaded guilty to murder, kidnapping and robbery, and while another, Aaron McKinney, awaits trial, national lesbian and gay organizations have focused the fear, anger, compassion and political capital aroused by Matthew Shepard's killing into a campaign for federal and state hate crimes legislation.

The Gay and Lesbian Alliance Against Defamation, the Human Rights Campaign (HRC), the National Gay and Lesbian Task Force (NGLTF), and Parents, Families and Friends of Lesbians And Gays, along with an assortment of religious, ethnic, feminist and civil rights groups, have all pursued hate crimes legislation. They are joined by President [Bill] Clinton, most Congressional Democrats and even a few Republicans, such as Senator Arlen Specter, who have endorsed the federal Hate Crimes Prevention Act (HCPA), a version of which failed to pass [1997's] Congress despite having more than 200 co-sponsors and some bipartisan support.

Hate crimes legislation denotes a set of prescriptions that include toughening sentencing guidelines, expanding federal jurisdiction and requiring the compilation of statistical data on bias crimes. (On the federal level, the Hate Crimes Statistics Act, passed in 1990, already requires the FBI to collect data on anti-LGBT violence.) Currently, twenty-one states and the District of Columbia have hate crimes laws with provisions on sexual orientation along with race, religion, ethnicity and, in some cases, disability and gender; twenty states have hate crimes laws that do not include sexual orientation, and nine states have no hate crimes laws whatsoever.

Hate Crime Law Is Not a Proven Deterrent

Even as national lesbian and gay organizations pursue hate crimes laws with single-minded fervor, concentrating precious resources and energy on these campaigns, there is no evidence that such laws actually prevent hate crimes. Passage of the federal HCPA would be largely symbolic: Although it would expand the potential for federal prosecution of anti-LGBT bias crimes, for the most part it would allow legislators to appear to be doing something about homophobia without actually addressing its cultural roots. Meanwhile, beneath the national radar, local antiviolence projects focused on community organizing, outreach and education—efforts that attempt to stop gay-bashing by changing the social environment in which it occurs—are struggling with scant resources.

Hate Crime Law Is Unlikely to Be Enforced

HRC and other national gay and lesbian organizations contend that if hate crimes laws are passed, law enforcement officials will not only report anti-LGBT violence but will also have the mandate and resources to prosecute it. Yet HRC's political director, Winnie Stachelberg, concedes that "local law enforcement agencies are often reluctant to report [such] crimes," and there is little reason to think that such reluctance would dissolve in the face of a new law. A 1998 report by the National Coalition of Anti-Violence Programs, a network of community-based organizations that monitor and respond to anti-LGBT violence, notes that instances of verbal harassment and abuse by police officers increased by 155 percent from 1997 to 1998, and reports of physical abuse by police grew by more than 866 percent. Given that law enforcement officials regularly harass gays and lesbians—and that antisodomy laws that enable such behavior are still on the books in eighteen states—it seems improbable that passage of hate crimes laws would suddenly transform the state into a guardian of gay and lesbian people.

Community antiviolence activists are intimately aware of this reality. In San Francisco, for example, Shawna Virago, a male-to-female transsexual activist with Community United Against Violence (CUAV), reports that law enforcement officials are not only indifferent to anti-LGBT violence but are often perpetrators of such acts. In 1998, she notes, 50 percent of reported incidents of violence against transgendered people in the Bay Area were committed by law enforcement officials. CUAV works alongside other antiviolence campaigns, such as the Bay Area Police Watch, youth groups and minority organizations, to compile its own statistical data on bias crimes; conduct educational workshops in public schools, social service agencies and police academies; create safer public spaces; and combat illegal strip searches of transgendered people by police officers. Given the pervasive homophobia of law enforcement agencies, these measures seem far better suited to the task of stemming anti-LGBT violence than hate crimes legislation.

In seeking federal prosecution and increased penalties for hate crimes, the NGLTF has argued that "criminal activity based on prejudice terrorizes not only victims but the entire community of which they are a part," and the HRC has said that "hate crimes affect more than just the individual attacked. . . . Hate crimes rend the fabric of society and fragment communities." Undoubtedly, lesbian, gay, bisexual and transgendered communities suffer fear and intimidation from violent assaults, but hate crimes laws are aimed at lengthening prison sentences, not creating safer community spaces.

Laws Will Not Erase Hate

Aaron McKinney and Russell Henderson, for instance, attacked Matthew Shepard at least in part to rob him, and McKinney attacked two Hispanic youths shortly after leaving Shepard for dead—making it clear that Shepard's murder occurred in the context of hostile racial and class relations, which hate crimes legislation would do nothing to address. In gentrifying or gentrified urban areas, such as New York's West Village, Chelsea and Park Slope, anti-LGBT violence occurs as existing populations are displaced by waves of lesbian and gay migration. Again, hate crimes legislation fails to grapple with this community problem.

Investing in local organizing, on the other hand, not only enables activists to connect the struggle against anti-gay and lesbian violence to such issues as job protection and the repeal of sodomy laws, it also builds gay and lesbian communities and creates safer social spaces—while at the same time reaching out to other communities to combat the problem of violence together. That's something no hate crimes law will ever do.

THE
HISTORY
OF
ISSUES

Hate Crimes in the Post-9/11 Era

Chapter Preface

On the morning of September 11, 2001, four American passenger airplanes were hijacked by terrorists who took over the cockpits. The first plane hit the North Tower of the World Trade Center at 8:46 in the morning. The plane hit floors 93 through 99 of the 110-story building. At the time of impact, the plane was moving at about 430 miles per hour and took out many of the tower's support columns. At 9:03, a second plane flew into the South Tower of the World Trade Center; images of the crash were caught by camera crews who had rushed to the site after the crash into the first tower. Because of the heavy news coverage, millions of people watched the second crash live on television. This plane hit floors 77 through 85 of the South Tower, also destroying many of the support columns. Fewer lives were claimed in the South Tower because of evacuation efforts made since the North Tower was hit, but the overall death toll (including the plane passengers) was still catastrophic.

At 9:37, a third plane crashed into a section of the Pentagon in Washington, D.C. As it turned out, this was an area of the Pentagon that was reinforced, had a sprinkler system, and was less populated than usual because of renovations. Although lives were tragically lost, the number could have been significantly higher. Meanwhile, phone calls from a fourth plane were made as passengers sought help against hijackers who claimed to have a bomb and had killed people on board. While making these calls to family members, passengers learned about the World Trade Center attacks.

At 9:47, the South Tower of the World Trade Center began to collapse from within. At the same time, a passenger aboard the fourth plane told his wife on the phone that the passengers voted to attempt a takeover. Calls placed shortly thereafter indicated that at least three passengers were forcing their way into the cockpit while other passengers jumped the hijacker guarding them; he claimed to have a bomb strapped to his body, but the passengers felt they had nothing to lose and had to try to prevent the hijackers from steering the plane into a building, causing greater casualties. At around 10:05, that plane crashed in a field in Pennsylvania, killing everyone on board.

At 9:59, the South Tower of the World Trade Center collapsed completely into a pile of smoking rubble. Fifteen minutes later, the damaged section of the Pentagon collapsed. About fifteen minutes after that, the North Tower collapsed completely. Much later in the day, at 5:20, World Trade Center Building Seven, a 47-story building also collapsed. It had been evacuated as a precaution, but the exact cause of its collapse is not known.

By the end of the day, those responsible for the attacks were identified as having been part of al Qaeda, a Middle Eastern terrorist group led by Arab Islamist Osama bin Laden. The death toll reached around 3,000 people, mostly civilians and emergency response workers. The attacks of September 11, on home soil, against innocent people going about their daily lives, shocked and terrified the entire nation.

The hate-motivated attacks of September 11 engendered a response that was also motivated in part by hate. In addition to experiencing grief and fear after the attacks, many Americans also felt anger, distrust, even hatred, toward anyone perceived to be Muslim or of Arabic descent. Many Arab Americans endured taunts, threats, and even physical violence. Amidst the heightened security at airports and other venues, those assumed to be of Middle Eastern heritage were often subjected to racial profiling, treated with increased suspicion because of their perceived ethnicity. While unsure how to improve the nation's security and prevent future attacks, a number of Americans spoke out against responding to the events of September 11 with still more hatred.

Limiting Rights and Profiling Are the Beginning of a Slippery Slope

Ed O'Brien

In the wake of the September 11, 2001, attacks on American soil, various programs were put in place to tighten security in an attempt to protect Americans from further harm. Because the terrorists on September 11 were Arab men who used airplanes to take American lives, racial profiling and monitoring were implemented, and airports changed their approach to security completely. While some found these measures both comforting and necessary, others saw them as unjust, dangerous, and conducive of an atmosphere of anxiety and mistrust. Critics of profiling have pointed to the potential for damage to society and race relations, and many have feared that if left unchecked, profiling and privacy invasions could lead to significant restrictions on human and legal rights in the United States.

In the following essay, Ed O'Brien warns that freedom itself is at stake in allowing profiling. Because it validates discrimination, it can only serve to hurt innocent people instead of protecting innocent people. O'Brien is the executive director and cofounder of Street Law, a nonprofit organization that educates people around the world about human fights and the law. In addition, O'Brien serves as an adjunct professor at Georgetown University, where he cofounded Human Rights USA and the Black South African Law Program.

It was September 29, [2001,] eighteen days after the terrible attacks on the World Trade Center and the Pentagon. While standing in a long luggage-check line with my daughter at

Ed O'Brien, "In War, Is Law Silent? Security and Freedom after September 11," *Social Education*, vol. 65, no. 7, 2001, pp. 419–25. Copyright © 2001 National Council for the Social Studies. Reprinted by permission.

Baltimore-Washington Airport—our first trip there since September 11—we noticed that a man who looked Middle Eastern had been pulled out of the line ahead. Both of his suitcases lay open on a table while airport security guards unpacked and searched them. He did not openly object, but on his face we could read his embarrassment at being singled out and having his clothes and personal effects exposed for all to see. The process took more than thirty minutes.

The trip to the airport that day took longer and was different for everyone. I had to park my car in a different spot, arrive two hours ahead of time for a domestic flight, and forgo talking with my daughter at the gate for the hour before the flight. Small things, one might say, but they all added up to a diminution in the freedom that my daughter and I had always enjoyed as Americans. But for people like the man whose luggage was searched—who may or may not have been Middle Eastern, and may or may not have been an American citizen—restrictions on freedoms and rights are in danger of going far beyond personal inconvenience.

Many Americans will cite the overriding need for security as an explanation for such occurrences. What happened on September 11 is unparalleled by anything we have ever known. The attacks killed more than 5,000 people, injured tens of thousands more, and caused economic hardship and grief to hundreds of thousands more. From the New York attacks alone, more than 10,000 people lost a parent. [In the year following the attacks, the casualty statistics were revised downward.] Millions more were traumatized by either watching the attacks directly or reliving them through hundreds of hours of replays or analysis. The hijackers trampled the victims' most basic human right—life—and destroyed the rights of people around the world to security. They made every person in this country afraid. Our right to feel safe has been limited in the short run, perhaps limited forever.

Weakened Human Rights

But how were other rights of Americans affected by this horrible event? Do all Americans now have fewer rights? Or only some Americans, people identified as "suspected terrorists" or "Arab-looking" or "Muslim"? If we agree that, because of September 11, the rights of some or all should be restricted, another vexing question arises: how much and for how long?

When we speak of "rights" in the United States, we usually refer to constitutional or legal rights: rights enforceable by law. But there is another category of rights, human rights. This term—originally known as natural rights—evolved from the theory that all people are entitled to certain protections and freedoms simply by virtue of being born human. These include the rights to food, shelter, bodily security, education, medical care, free press, free speech, and freedom of religion, among others. Eleanor Roosevelt led the movement to encourage the nations of the world to formally agree to respect these rights. Her vision came true in 1948 when the United Nations adopted the Universal Declaration of Human Rights. Today, most nations accept, at least in theory, the concept of human rights as inalienable and agree that they should not be limited by any government or people. . . .

Wartime Changes Legal Perspectives

There is a Latin expression, "Inter arma silent leges," meaning that "in war, laws are silent." Commenting on this, U.S. Supreme Court Chief Justice William Rehnquist has stated a slightly different view. In his book [*All the Laws but One: Civil Liberties in Wartime*, 1998], which examines the question of what rights the courts have allowed in the past, he says that laws during wartime are not silent, but "they speak in a somewhat different voice."

During war, great deference is usually given to the executive branch, but today's war is a "war against terrorism," not a traditional war against one or more countries. Because of this lack of clarity as to who exactly "the enemy" is, restricting the rights of a particular nationality or religious group may be both ineffective and unconstitutional.

The random action and indiscriminate assaults and killing that have marked terrorism in the late twentieth and early twenty-first centuries naturally make people call for heightened security. These cries for increased exercise of authority and control conflict with our notions of civil liberties and human rights.

Current proposals and new practices and policies will certainly have an effect on the freedom and privacy of travelers. Closely related to this is the possibility that racial and ethnic profiling will be tolerated in practice (even if profiling is not considered right in principle) in measures aimed at ensuring the safety of travelers and in initiatives to investigate terrorism.

A major question is the extent to which citizens' rights of privacy will be challenged by new measures of surveillance aimed at preventing or investigating acts of terrorism. A critical issue in this regard is whether such surveillance will be conducted very broadly or whether it will need to be justified on the ground that it is aimed at specific targets in clearly defined circumstances. Whatever the case, visitors to the United States and immigrants who are not citizens are likely to be even more affected by these measures than U.S. citizens.

Airports and Airplanes

The atmosphere in airports and aboard planes is already different and is likely never to be as open and free as before. Many people say that the events of September 11 were caused by lax airport and airplane security, and if changes are made, hijackings can at least be reduced, if not stopped. Plans have been proposed to federalize some security staff in airports, especially those who operate the bag scanners and metal detectors. These employees—the majority of whom have been estimated to be non-citizens—have long been underpaid and undertrained.

Following September 11, most American travelers seem willing to accept the increased time at the airport if we get better security, but how many restrictions on our rights will we put up with? Would we accept the kind of security that is common at Ben-Gurion Airport in Tel Aviv, [Israel,] where passengers are routinely asked personal questions about where they have been, what they did, and where they are going? Refusal to answer often results in missed flights. Would Americans put up with eye, facial, voice, and fingerprint recognition tests? Some security companies and politicians are proposing just such measures. Would we endure occasional strip searches or the total unpacking of suitcases by inspectors? Should all travelers be subject to these measures, or only certain people? One thing is clear: airports will never be the same again.

Airplanes will never be the same, either. After September 11, President [George W.] Bush ordered that the National Guard be stationed at many airports. The federal government is already putting armed federal marshals aboard many airplanes. They may become a permanent fixture in air travel. Cockpit doors are being fitted with stronger locks and may be sealed during flights. Some groups propose that pilots be armed with either pistols or stun guns. Passengers are no longer allowed to bring on board knives or sharp instruments, such as razors, tweezers, scissors, or box cutters. Items that could double as weapons must be stored, left at home, or checked in a suitcase. To date, little or no protest has occurred over these inconveniences. Time will tell to what extent and for how long passengers will accept these restrictions, but it seems likely that more will be implemented.

Racial and Ethnic Profiling

One of the most controversial issues arising from the freedom-versus-security debate concerns racial and ethnic profiling. In this profiling, law enforcement officials subject persons of a particular race or ethnicity to searches, questioning, detainment, or other measures to which the larger population is not subjected, when there are not other suspicious circumstances against the person. Critics say that it violates whole groups' rights to privacy, equal protection under the law, security, and protection against illegal searches. In recent years, many African Americans have felt singled out and harassed by police for the "crime" of "DWB" (driving while black). Studies have verified that this practice has taken place, and in some instances, courts and police commissioners have ordered the practice stopped. In the aftermath of September 11, both President Bush and [then] Attorney General [John] Ashcroft have spoken out against racial and ethnic profiling and said that they would work at the federal level to crack down on it if it occurred.

All terrorists, even the majority of terrorists, are not Arabs, Middle Eastern, or Muslim. In fact, of the 87 terrorist incidents in the United States between 1984 and 1998, only two were linked to an Arab group. Just as very few Christians are extremists and perform violent acts, such as bombing abortion clinics, only a tiny proportion of Arabs are extremists, and only a minute number of extremists are terrorists.

Since September 11, however, some officials have singled out this broad group for racial and ethnic profiling, including people who may look like they are from the Middle East. Unfortunately, Americans are not often well-educated about different countries and cultures, though our population includes people from every corner of the globe. Since September 11, many Americans have been looking askance at Indians (especially Sikhs, who wear beards and turbans), Pakistanis, or people of myriad other ethnic backgrounds and nationalities, believing them to be Arabs and therefore suspicious. Arab Americans and people of other ethnic backgrounds have had property vandalized and destroyed; adults and children have been harassed and beaten up. The same treatment has been inflicted on Muslims of a number of ethnicities—Muslims from Central Europe and all parts of Asia and Africa, as well as American Muslims.

Lumping all Muslims in the United States with a small extremist group whose violent acts violate all the basic tenets of Islam is wrong. But many Americans are doing it, which means that they are violating the rights of others in a country whose cornerstone is freedom. Visiting a mosque in Virginia two weeks after September 11, I was told of many instances of profiling and discrimination, including an instance where a Muslim woman wearing the hijab (head-scarf) was confronted on the street by a white man, who ripped off her veil and threw it in a nearby trash can, while bystanders looked on. To his credit, six days after the terror, President Bush visited a mosque and spoke out against such acts. "The face of terror is not the true face of Islam; Islam is peace." (In fact, the word Islam is derived from the word meaning "peace" in Arabic.) Recalling a similar story, President Bush also said that the women who cover their heads should not fear leaving their homes. "That's not the America I know," he said. "That should not and that will not stand in America."

Arab Americans Feel Heightened Discrimination

Three weeks after the attacks, I interviewed Jean AbiNader, managing director of the Arab American Institute (AAI), which represents Arab American interests in government and politics in the United States. He told me that during the three weeks since the attacks, AAI had received 420 complaints of discrimination, many times the number of complaints the group ever before received during a similar time period. In his view, the biggest impact on Arab Americans may be on their right to move freely, especially by plane. Some staffers in his own organization were unable to do their jobs, which required travel, because of fears of harassment by other passengers or airline officials. We have all read the newspaper reports of such incidents as a pilot telling an Arab American passenger that unless he got off the plane, he would not fly it. Many Arab Americans fear being subjected to the suspicions of other passengers and the crew.

At the same time, AbiNader expressed appreciation for the fact that many Americans and U.S. organizations are reaching out to the Arab American community. He told me that the community had been very impressed by the support given it by administration officials, including the President and Attorney General, against hostility, violence and discrimination after September 11.

Although the President, the Attorney General, and many others have said that racial and ethnic profiling are wrong, airlines are under tremendous pressure to prevent future hijackings. Some say that in this instance, such profiling is reasonable and justifiable. On a recent television show author William F. Buckley said, "It makes sense to check Arabs who are traveling. It is less likely that a non-Arab-looking person is going to hijack an airplane." Neil Livingstone, an expert on terrorism security with Global Options, an international risk management firm, said recently that "ethnicity is the single most important determinant of who is going to cause a problem on an airplane. If you are going to give the same attention, because it is mandated, to a little old lady with blue hair, or to a young African American . . . as you give to a Middle Easterner, you are undermining the system already."

But other security experts, such as Raymond Kelly, a former New York City Police Commissioner and U.S. Customs Commissioner, disagree. Kelly says that other factors, such as place of birth, length of time spent in the United States, and country of origin, are just as important as ethnic background. Although gathering such data on all passengers will infringe on everyone's privacy rights, perhaps it is better than singling out many millions who may, in a security person's eyes, "look" Middle Eastern or Arab.

One thing to keep in mind, however, if we pass laws or make policies that allow for the restrictions of the rights of certain groups, is that we may be going down a slippery slope. Today we might decide that it is worthwhile to limit Arab Americans' rights. Tomorrow, another group of Americans worried about the Mafia or the contemporary drug trade might feel it [is] in the interests of national security to restrict the rights of Italian Americans or Colombian Americans. With the Arab American example as a precedent, such measures might become easier and easier to put into effect.

All of us want to be treated with dignity—the basis of all human rights. Whether security personnel use dignified or undignified methods to single out people for extensive searches, questioning, or other restrictions will make a big difference in the extent to which we allow racial and ethnic profiling and rights restrictions in the future. . . .

Freedom vs. Security

The extent to which American rights become more limited as a result of the current "war on terrorism" will depend on how long it lasts and how much more terrorism occurs on American soil.

Americans seem to be of two minds in the debate between freedom and security. They want to be left alone and yet they want to be protected. They do realize that they are likely to relinquish some freedom; in a poll taken during the month following the attacks, eight out of ten Americans said that they believed that they would have to give up some of their personal freedom to make the country safe from terrorism. The debate in Congress after September 11 showed hesitancy among many lawmakers, both Democrats and Republicans, when limiting the rights of Americans in the name of security. At the end of October, however, Congress passed compromise legislation providing for restrictions on the rights of those suspected of terrorism.

Do we have to choose between freedom and security, or can we find a balance? Often in our constitutional history, we have negotiated this balance best when we tried to include the interests of both sides while keeping true to the country's founding values. This may be what George F. Kennan, former U.S. ambassador to Russia and one of the most knowledgeable people about the Cold War, meant fifty years ago when he wrote that the fear of communism could turn us "intolerant, suspicious, cruel, and terrified of internal dissension because we have lost our own belief in ourselves and in the power of our ideals." We will not be defending democracy if we abandon basic democratic values in the pursuit of our security.

Stereotyping and Targeting Arabs Only Fuels Fear and Violence

Susan M. Akram

While reports suggest a rise in attacks against Arab Americans since the terrorist strikes on September 11, negative portrayals of Arabs existed in the United States long before the tragedy in 2001. A negative stereotype of Arabs and Muslims could be found in many aspects of American culture, portraying them as untrustworthy and unfeeling. Many observers contend that through media and film portrayals, along with government policies, a preexisting tacit endorsement of mistreating Arabs laid the foundation for a backlash after September 11.

In the following viewpoints, Susan M. Akram describes in detail the way the entertainment industry has traditionally portrayed Arabs and Muslims. She also discusses the cultural effects of past government policies to strip Arabs of their rights under the umbrella of security. Akram is an associate clinical professor at the Boston University School of Law.

The demonizing of Arabs and Muslims in America began well before the terrible tragedy of September 11, 2001. It can be traced to deliberate mythmaking by film and media, stereotyping as part of conscious strategy of 'experts' and polemicists on the Middle East, the selling of a foreign policy agenda by US government officials and groups seeking to affect that agenda, and a public susceptible to images identifying the unwelcome 'other' in its midst. Bearing the brunt of these factors are Arab and Muslim non-citizens in this country. A series of government laws and policies since the 1970's have steadily targeted Arab and Muslim non-citizens for selec-

Susan M. Akram, "The Aftermath of September 11, 2001: The Targeting of Arabs and Muslims in America," *Arab Studies Quarterly*, 2002. Reproduced by permission.

tive interrogation, detention, harassment, presumption of terrorist involvement, and removal from this country. The Patriot Act, recent round-up and detention of over 1,000 and [a] list of interrogation targets of 5,000 individuals, and the Presidential Order to establish quasi-military 'tribunals' exacerbate the selective targeting of Arab and Muslim non-citizens in a climate of fear that completely sanctions blatant racial profiling.

Stereotyping Arabs as Terrorists and Religious Fanatics

Commentators fit anti-Arab, anti-Muslim animus into various 'racist' theories, from anti-immigrant sentiment that targets whichever group represents the most recent immigrant population to a more dynamic process of 'racialization' that focuses on a social-political order that requires a marginalized 'other'. The former only partly explains the demonizing of Arabs and Muslims in America, especially as Arabs (not necessarily Muslims) in particular have been part of the fabric of United States society since the late 1800s. The latter, [Michael] Omi and [Howard] Winant's characterization, is more helpful, but does not precisely delineate the very specific factors that have come together to 'racialize' Arabs and Muslims in the United States. Still, the reasons for defining race as a process are particularly valid, as they indicate both the severe damage 'racialization' can do to the communities and individuals affected, and that the process can be reversed. Social or historical analysts focusing on the problem have identified how and why Arabs and Muslims in particular have been racialized in America:

> Anti-Arab racism does not emanate from a single source, and certainly is not limited to passions stemming from the Arab-Israeli conflict. Several types of anti-Arab racism and violence can be discerned. The first, and most obvious, is the political violence of Jewish extremist groups, which is

correctly viewed as emanating from the Arab-Israeli
conflict. . . . The second is a more nativistic violence which
is xenophobic and local in nature. . . . The third is a form of
jingoist hostility and violence usually associated with international crises involving U.S. citizens [according to Nabeel
Abraham]. . . .

Nabeel Abraham is not alone in identifying these sources
of anti-Arab and anti-Muslim racism, but his work is particularly helpful in marshalling evidence to corroborate each factor. His second factor is better viewed as including xenophobia fed by film and media stereotypes about Arabs and
Muslims. His third factor is also more accurately broadened to
include hostility and violence related to foreign or domestic
crises in which U.S. citizens are seen as victims. To his list,
however, must be added a fourth factor, which is deliberate
misinformation, distortion and institutionalized racism existing in government, law enforcement and influential institutions that target Arabs and Muslims both within the U.S. and
abroad. . . .

Anti-Arab Xenophobia and Demonizing Images in Media

The popular caricature of the average Arab is as mythical as
the old portrait of the Jew.

He is robed and turbaned, sinister and dangerous, engaged
mainly in hijacking airplanes and blowing up public build-
ings. It seems that the human race cannot discriminate between a tiny minority of persons who may be objectionable
and the ethnic strain from which they spring. If the Italians
have the Mafia, all Italians are suspect; if the Jews have finan-
ciers, all Jews are part of an international conspiracy; if the
Arabs have fanatics, all Arabs are violent. In the world today,
more than ever, barriers of this kind must be broken, for we
are all more alike than we are different.

In his work on anti-Arab racism, Abraham has studied lo-
calized racism and violence that does not emanate from a par-

ticular hate group or organization with a political/ideological agenda. This type of anti-Arab/anti-Muslim hostility is not necessarily related to the Arab-Israeli conflict, U.S. foreign policy, or particular events in the Middle East, but is, of course, exacerbated by any or all of these factors. Abraham has focused on the Arab and Muslim communities of the greater Detroit area, because of the increase in such xenophobic-driven violence in areas where Arabs are highly visible. He has documented a huge range of hate messages, discrimination and violence directed at Arabs, both from private citizens and from town, state and other officials. As examples, mayoral candidate, Michael Guido distributed a brochure in Dearborn, a Detroit suburb, in which he claimed the city's Arab-Americans "threaten our neighborhoods, the value of our property and a darned good way of life." In 1981, Michigan governor William Milliken, said in a newspaper interview that Michigan's economic woes were due to the "damn Arabs." Such statements and campaigns by public officials fuel the perception that violence against this 'other' community is acceptable.

Feeding already-existing stereotypes in American society about Arabs and Muslims, media and film have found a ready audience for dangerous and one-dimensional images. Jack Shaheen's meticulous work [*Reel Bad Arabs: How Hollywood Vilifies a People*, 2001] reviewing 900 Hollywood films over a period of four years is the most convincing evidence of deliberate vilifying of Arabs and Muslims by the movie industry. Hollywood has made hundreds of movies in which Arabs or Muslims are portrayed as terrorists or dishonest sub-humans. According to Shaheen, there are only five Arab 'types': villains, sheikhs, maidens, Egyptians and Palestinians. Arab women are portrayed primarily in two roles: as weak and mute, covered in black, or as scantily clad belly dancers. There are three and one half million Americans of Arab heritage, yet Jack Shaheen was able to find Arabs portrayed in a favorable light in only five percent of the 900 Hollywood films he reviewed, and only a handful in which Arabs had leading roles as protagonists. According to Shaheen, part of the explanation also lies in a political agenda: one-seventh of all films made since the 1970's have been shot in Israel or made by Israeli teams. Moreover, the U.S. Department of Defense has cooperated with Hollywood in making over 14 films showing American soldiers killing Arabs or Muslims.

Nor has Islam fared any better on the silver screen. Islam is inextricably linked with 'holy war', male patriarchy, and terrorism. Arab Muslims are shown as hostile invaders, or 'lecherous oil sheikhs intent on using nuclear weapons'. A far-too-common scene shows a mosque with Arabs at prayer, cutting away to showing civilians being gunned down.

Most important about film portrayals of Arabs and Muslims is the omission of Arabs as ordinary people, families with social interactions, or outstanding members of communities such as scholars or writers or scientists. Stereotyping and demonizing of the Arab or Muslim by American film has been so complete and so successful that film critics, most Americans and social commentators have barely noticed.

"Patriotic" Racism

There is a well-documented high correlation between international or domestic crises in which American citizens are seen as victims of foreign aggression and an increase in hostility towards non-white, non-Christian people [in] the U.S. Perpetrators of hostile acts or aggression in such situations do not appear to differentiate among victims—they target brown-skinned people of any religion or ethnic origin, from Pakistanis, Indians, Iranians and Japanese to Muslims, Sikhs and Christian Arabs. However, the public perception of "Arabs" as responsible for most terrorism against Americans and American interests results in Arab-Americans feeling the greatest impact of this hostility. One can readily track the causal relationship between international crises involving 'Arabs' and Arab-bashing here at home.

Taking only the 1980's to the present, there is a plethora of evidence to document this cause-effect relationship. On June 14, 1985, TWA flight 847 was highjacked to Beirut by Lebanese Shi'ite gunmen. One young American was beaten to death on the plane, and the 39 remaining passengers were detained for 17 days before being released. In the wake of a huge media reaction and sensationalist print and live journalism, there was an outbreak of violent attacks on Arab-Americans and U.S. residents of Middle Eastern origin around the country. In June, Islamic Centers in San Francisco, Denver, Dearborn and Quincy, Massachusetts, were either vandalized or threatened, as were Arab-American organizations in New York and Detroit. A Houston mosque was firebombed. In August, a bomb placed in the door of the ADC [American-Arab Anti-Discrimination Committee] in Boston detonated, severely injuring two policemen. The same pattern was repeated in the fall of 1985, when the *Achille Lauro* cruise liner was hijacked and Leon Klinghoffer was killed. A wave of anti-Arab violence ensued in the U.S., including the bombing of the Los Angeles ADC office, in which the director, Alex Odeh was killed.

Again in 1986, in apparent response to the [Ronald] Reagan Administration's 'war on terrorism', at the time directed at Libya, another episode of anti-Arab hysteria broke out. The same night of the U.S. raid on Libya, the national ADC office in Washington received threats indicating ADC has some connection with Libya. The Detroit ADC office, the Dearborn Arab community center and the Dearborn Arab-American newspaper all received bomb threats. Beatings and other violent attacks on Arabs were reported around the U.S. One of the incidents reported was that of a Palestinian immigrant family whose house was broken into and a smoke bomb thrown inside, with the words "Go Back to Libya" scrawled on the walls.

The Gulf War intensified anti-Arab hostility in the United States. Before the invasion of Kuwait in 1990, ADC had recorded five anti-Arab hate crimes for the year. Immediately after the invasion, from August 2, 1990, until February 2, 1991, ADC recorded 86 incidents. The reports noted that 56 percent of the incidents targeted Arab-American organizations, political activists and dissenters of US foreign policy. When U.S. intervention began in January 1991, Arab and Muslim community organizations were bombed, vandalized or subjected to harassment from one part of the country to the other. Arab-owned businesses were vandalized or destroyed by arson in many states.

In the 1980's, the government initiated a series of new policies to silence Arab-American and Arab immigrants' political speech and activism under the guise of fighting 'terrorism'. These policies might have more serious long-term consequences than sporadic, although individually devastating, private acts of anti-Arab/Muslim violence. Events since September 11 have exacerbated all the factors underlying the racializing of Arabs in America, with predictable results.

Institutionalized Racism

One of the factors with the greatest impact on the targeting of Arabs and Muslims is what might best be termed 'institutionalized racism' in government and law enforcement, in collaboration with institutions and think-tanks having a specific ideological or foreign policy agenda driven by anti-Arabism. This is also possibly the least well-documented phenomenon in the racializing of Arabs and Muslims leading to the widespread acceptance of profiling and related loss of civil liberties. Although this article focuses primarily on post-1990 events, institutionalized racism within U.S. government agencies began long before then. One can pinpoint the initiation of the [Richard] Nixon Administration's "Operation Boulder" as perhaps the first concerted U.S. government effort to target

Arabs in the U.S. for special investigation with the specific purpose of intimidation, harassment, and to discourage their activism on issues relating to the Middle East. "Operation Boulder" comprised a series of Presidential directives issued by President Nixon, ostensibly to deal with the terrorist threat posed by the Munich Olympics hostage-taking and its bloody outcome. The directives authorized the FBI to investigate individuals of 'Arabic-speaking origin,' supposedly to determine their potential relationship with 'terrorist' activities related to the Arab-Israeli conflict. It is important to note that at that period of time, the only terrorist acts in the U.S. related to the Arab-Israeli conflict had been committed by the JDL [Jewish Defense League]. Later investigations, both by the press and by organizations in the Arab-American community, confirmed that "Operation Boulder" was initiated as a result of pressure from Zionist groups both within the U.S. and from Israel to silence Arab-Americans from voicing opposition to U.S. and Israeli policies in the Middle East. Under "Operation Boulder", the FBI investigated, interrogated and intimidated non-citizens and citizens only of Arab origin, often in early-morning visits, without making formal charges of any kind. The most striking case that emerged from this period was the wiretapping and surveillance of prominent Detroit lawyer Abdeen Jabara, then-President of the Association of Arab-American University Graduates. The Associated Press reported the investigation of Jabara as follows:

> The US Justice Department admits it repeatedly used electronic devices to eavesdrop on Detroit lawyer Abdeen Jabara. . . . In a statement filed Tuesday in a US district court in Detroit, the Federal Bureau of Investigation (FBI) and Justice Department admitted the surveillance of said information about Jabara was handed over to Jewish, Zionist or Israeli organizations. The admission came in response to questions growing out of a lawsuit filed by Jabara in October, 1972. . . .

In the 1980's, the Reagan Administration also used foreign policy 'imperatives' selectively to target Arabs in the U.S. for harassment and intimidation, again on the grounds of combating terrorism. In early January 1986, President Reagan publicly began laying the foundation for striking against Libya in supposed retaliation for Arab terrorist attacks at the Rome and Vienna airports that had resulted in multiple deaths and injuries. Reagan announced that the U.S. government had "irrefutable" evidence that Libyan leader Muammar Qaddafi was responsible, and in August 1981, the U.S. Navy shot down two Libyan planes off the Gulf of Sidra as part of US 'war games.' President Reagan also announced that "we have the evidence" that Qaddafi was sending hit teams to assassinate him. In fact, the U.S. government as well as foreign governments apparently were aware that there was no evidence that Qaddafi was behind the terrorist attacks in Rome and Vienna or that any Libyan 'hit squads' had been sent to the U.S. According to the FBI, there was also no evidence connecting Libya to the hijacking of a Rome to Athens TWA flight or the bombing of a West Berlin nightclub, but the U.S. carried out bombing raids against Libya nevertheless. The other consequence of the disinformation campaign was a rash of vandalism and violence against U.S. residents of Arab or Middle Eastern origin and their community centers, mosques, businesses and homes.

In the 1990's, after the invasion of Kuwait, Iraq and Saddam Hussein became the focus of the first Bush Administration's 'war on terrorism.' Creating a climate in which anti-Arab sentiment was inevitable, the Administration called the Iraqi leader Saddam Hussein "the new Hitler of the Middle East," accusing Iraqi forces of atrocities against Kuwaitis, many which later proved to be fabricated. Of far greater significance for Arab-Americans' civil rights, however, was the Administration's decision to launch massive surveillance against Arabs in America. The FBI initiated a nationwide interrogation effort against Arab-American community leaders, activists and others, particularly harassing antiwar demonstrators. Additional policy measures put in place were nationwide fingerprinting of all residents and immigrants in the U.S. of Arab origin, and the institution of an FAA [Federal Aviation Administration] system of airline profiling targeting individuals from the Arab world. Private harassment and violence against the Arab and Muslim communities was exacerbated by these government policies targeting the selfsame communities. . . .

The Aftermath of the 9/11 Terrorist Attacks

The devastating terrorist attack of 9-11 caused a familiar and predictable response in the United States on two fronts: government policies specifically targeting Arabs and Muslims; and nationwide violence against Arabs and Muslims. As the government stepped up its "war on terror", the Administration and federal agencies put in place one set of policies after another that focused on the Arab and Muslim communities. . . .

Within weeks, the U.S. government arrested and detained over 1,200 Muslim and Arab non-citizens. Although the roundup included Arab and Muslim men from many countries, the majority was from Pakistan and Egypt. None of these individuals were found to have any direct links with the terrorists or their actions. Approximately 100 of them were charged with minor crimes, and another approximately 500 were held in custody on immigration violations such as overstaying temporary nonimmigrant visas. Attorney General [John] Ashcroft stated publicly that minor immigration charges would be used to detain non-citizens while the criminal investigation continued.

Repercussions of Anti-Arab Sentiment in Post-9/11 America

In many ways, the post 9-11 dragnet resembles the Japanese internment during World War II because, instead of individualized suspicion, statistical probabilities are being used to target discrete and insular minorities who are being classified as enemy aliens. Loyalty and national identity are thus being defined by 'foreign' appearance, whatever that may mean to the particular officer or agency in charge of the decision. This has grave consequences, not only for the civil liberties of Arabs and Muslims, but for all citizens who are members of minority groups. Similar concerns affect U.S. citizens, as their rights to confidentiality and privacy are eroded by government rules that violate fundamental notions of fair trial such as attorney-client privileged communication, open trials and hearings, the right to confront adverse government information, access to government records under the Freedom of Information Act, and limits on detention. These fundamental rights are being eroded for non-citizens and citizens alike.

Weak immigration laws were not the problem before 9-11; arguably, enforcement was. The terrorists were able to enter the U.S. and remain, not because of insufficient legal safeguards, but because of INS [Immigration and Naturalization Service] and other agency inefficiencies in implementing existing laws. Mohammad Atta [one of the 9/11 hijackers], for example, was admitted as a tourist. On entry, INS inspectors learned he planned to attend pilot training school—something he needed a student visa for. INS agents in Florida questioned him, saw that he had the wrong visa, but allowed him entry. Neither Congress nor the Administration has made a convincing argument that law before 9-11 was insufficient to prevent the hijackers from entering the U.S. or getting on airplanes. Under the broader definition of *terrorist* in the Patriot Act, the 9-11 hijackers would not have been screened out because they had no previous criminal history, and had not announced their intention of attacking anyone. In contrast, the new provision will deny visas to broad classes of aliens who will now be ineligible for adjustment of status, release pending deportation, asylum and withholding of removal, with no more than an urebutted presumption on the part of the government that they were associated with someone engaging in terrorist activity. Anyone who has been involved in a knife fight will be inadmissible under the new law. No more than prior law, the Patriot Act will not make immigration officers mind readers, to be able to determine what an individual with no past criminal history plans to do on entering the United States.

The government's actions in the 'war on terrorism' after 9-11 do not appear to meaningfully enhance the security of the American people against terrorism. They are, on the other hand, exacting an extraordinarily high price on Arab and Muslim non-citizens, already demonized through historical animosity by private and government groups and individuals. They are, indeed, rapidly eroding the civil liberties of other non-citizens and U.S. citizens as well.

Hate Crimes Against Arabs Have Increased in Post-9/11 America

Riad Z. Abdelkarim

After the September 11, 2001, attacks, Americans were devastated, and many felt threatened. Patriotic feeling was heightened as citizens felt bonded by a crisis inflicted upon them by outsiders. Because those outsiders shared the same ethnicity, many others of that ethnicity came under suspicion. Many Arabs in the United States felt the hostility and mistrust of other Americans, attitudes based solely on their shared ethnicity with the attackers. In some cases, the hostility was so pronounced that it manifested in violence. Fear turned to hate, and hate turned to hate crimes. Government policies to protect American soil only added fuel to the fire as they seemed to endorse discrimination and the compromising of rights.

Physician and writer Riad Z. Abdelkarim is a Muslim activist in Anaheim, California. He has written extensively on the Arab-American experience, especially with regard to the September 11 attacks and the Iraqi War. He serves as a communications director for the Council on American-Islamic Relations.

For Arabs and Muslims living, working, and going to school in the United States, the end of 2002 and the beginning of 2003 were marked by poignant reminders of the unease and apprehension that has permeated their communities in the ongoing aftermath of the Sept. 11, 2001 terrorist attacks. First, the FBI released its annual hate crimes report for 2001, which showed a marked increase in hate crimes targeting Muslims

Riad Z. Abdelkarim, "Surge in Hate Crimes Followed by Official U.S. Targeting of Muslim, Arab Men," *Washington Report on Middle East Affairs*, vol. 22, no. 3, April 2003. Copyright © 2003 American Educational Trust. All rights reserved. Reproduced by permission.

and people who are or appear to be of Middle Eastern or South Asian descent. Then, the INS [Immigration and Naturalization Service] announced a controversial new "special registration" process for non-immigrant visa holders from predominantly Muslim and Arab countries. That move rekindled concerns among these communities of unfair ethnic and religious profiling.

The FBI report found that incidents targeting people, institutions and businesses identified with the Islamic faith increased from a mere 28 in 2000 to 481 in 2001—a rise of 1,600 percent.

Although the statistics did not specify the dates on which the 481 incidents occurred, the FBI theorized in somewhat understated fashion that the increased attacks were "presumably . . . a result of the heinous incidents that occurred on Sept. 11." According to the report, most of the incidents against Muslims and people who are or were believed to be of Middle Eastern ethnicity involved assaults and intimidation. Three cases of murder or manslaughter and 35 cases of arson also were reported, however.

Unfortunately, as disturbing as these statistics are, the numbers of hate crimes reported by the FBI most likely vastly underestimate the true number of incidents that took place, as many Muslims are believed not to have reported such incidents to law enforcement authorities. According to statistics gathered by the Council on American-Islamic Relations (CAIR), a national Muslim civil rights and advocacy group, as of February 2002 the number of hate crimes and "anti-Muslim" incidents reported by American Muslims exceeded 1,700. These ranged from public harassment and hate mail to bomb threats, death threats, physical assault, property damage, and murder.

U.S. Government Response to Anti-Muslim Sentiment

One question that has arisen in the aftermath of this surge in hate crimes is whether the U.S. government responded appropriately to the post-911 environment of anti-Muslim hysteria. The answer is both yes and no, according to a report by Human Rights Watch (HRW), entitled *We Are Not the Enemy: Hate Crimes Against Arabs, Muslims, and Those Perceived to Be Arab or Muslim After September 11.*

"Government officials didn't sit on their hands while Muslims and Arabs were attacked after Sept. 11," said Amardeep Singh, author of the report and U.S. Program researcher at Human Rights Watch. "But law enforcement and other government agencies should have been better prepared for this kind of onslaught."

The HRW report praises the official condemnation of hate crimes after Sept. 11 by public figures, including President George W. Bush. It notes, however, that "the U.S. government contradicted its anti-prejudice message by directing its anti-terrorism efforts—including secret immigration detention and FBI interviews of thousands of non-citizens—at Arabs and Muslims."

Government Profiling Reinforces Suspicion

Indeed, after the initial wave of hate crimes against American Muslims and Arab-Americans, a second manifestation of the post-9/11 backlash ensued. Sadly, this backlash was in large part sanctioned by and carried out by our own government. It is interesting to note that one category of incidents compiled by CAIR—not to be found in the FBI report—is "FBI/Police/INS Intimidation," with a total of 224 reported cases. As HRW's Singh notes, "Since Sept. 11, a pall of suspicion has been cast over Arabs and Muslims in the United States. Public officials can help reduce bias violence against them by ensuring that the 'war against terrorism' is focused on criminal behavior rather than whole communities."

This "pall of suspicion" has been extended further with the INS's controversial new "special registration" program, which overwhelmingly targets non-immigrant visa holders from

Muslim and Arab countries. Attorney General John Ashcroft initially announced the new program, the National Security Entry-Exit Registration System (NSEERS), in June 2002.

At that time, Ashcroft claimed the new program would "expand substantially America's scrutiny of those foreign visitors who may present an elevated national security risk." NSEERS requires non-immigrant visitors from countries deemed to be of "highest terrorism risk" to register with the U.S. government and be photographed and fingerprinted. The Justice Department estimated that between 100,000 to 200,000 visitors would be subject to the registration program.

Civil liberties groups, some members of Congress, and Arab and Muslim American groups immediately criticized the program, saying it singled out Muslims from Middle Eastern countries.

"It's pretty obvious that this plan won't work at anything except allowing the government to essentially 'pick on' people who haven't done anything wrong but happen to come from the administration's idea of the wrong side of the global tracks," said Lucas Guttentag, director of the American Civil Liberties Union (ACLU) Immigrants' Rights Project. "Selective enforcement of any law based on unchangeable characteristics like race, ethnicity or national origin is at its core un-American."

First Round of NSEERS Registration

The first registration deadline was Dec. 16, 2002, and targeted males aged 16 and over from Iran, Iraq, Syria, Libya and Sudan. That date did not pass uneventfully. In Southern California, hundreds of men and teenage boys were arrested at INS offices as they voluntarily tried to comply with the new regulations. Many of these were Iranians—students, professionals, and others—as California is home to an estimated 600,000 Persians. Relatives who accompanied their male family members to INS offices in Southern California, expecting a

10- to 15-minute registration process as promised by the INS, instead left the offices sobbing and without their loved ones.

INS officials stated that those detained were held on immigration violation charges. Many of these had nearly completed the process for legal residency; others were in the midst of asylum or status adjustment applications. Although the Department of Justice and the INS refused to say how many people had been apprehended in California or around the country, estimates were as high as 1,000 in Southern California alone. Some immediately posted bail and were released pending deportation hearings. Others, however, languished for days in crowded, unsanitary conditions where some claimed harsh treatment from authorities.

Mistreatment of Registrants

Civil rights groups, and Arab, Muslim, and Iranian-American groups and leaders immediately cried foul. Ramona Ripston, executive director of the ACLU's Southern California chapter, described the arrests as "shocking," and reminiscent of the internment of Japanese-Americans during World War II. Other community leaders ridiculed the government's contention that the special registration process improved the security of our nation. "Terrorists most likely wouldn't come to the INS to register," scoffed Sabiha Khan of the Southern California chapter of CAIR. And Peter Schey, president of the Los Angeles-based Center for Human Rights and Constitutional Law, contended that "No undocumented terrorist would come forward. . . . The program is being used as a scam to lure people into INS offices supposedly to register, when what they really face is arrest, detention and even deportation."

Two days after the initial deadline and mass detentions, thousands of people—mostly Iranian-Americans—rallied in front of the Westwood Federal Building in Los Angeles. Some carried signs that read: "What's next? Concentration camps?"; "Detain terrorists, not innocent immigrants" and "Free our fathers, brothers, husbands and sons." Kayhan Shakib, president of the Iranian-American Lawyers Association, which helped organize the protest, said the INS was not adequately prepared to handle the hundreds of people who went there to register on the day of the deadline, resulting in the unnecessary detainment of individuals.

Later the same week, hundreds of community members attended an Orange County town hall meeting hosted by CAIR and cosponsored by other community organizations, where they heard such speakers as the wife of one detained man cry while she described her family's ordeal. Meanwhile Stephen Thorn, a federal mediator with the Justice Department's Community Relations Service, was flown down from Sacramento to address the concerns of an increasingly angry Iranian-American community. His comments to about 40 community leaders are representative of the apparent intimidation tactics currently undertaken by the Justice Department. "I understand that there have been some demonstrations and some marches," Thorn stated, then warned of the "negative effect" of such demonstrations. "It makes other people think you don't want to be here," he said. "I think we need to look at what is the impact of open, glaring challenges to our system."

The following week, four national organizations filed a class action lawsuit against Attorney General Ashcroft and immigration officials, asking for an injunction to prevent the INS from further detaining individuals in the process of applying for residency. The lawsuit was filed by the Arab-American Anti-Discrimination Committee (ADC), Alliance of Iranian-Americans, CAIR, and the National Council of Pakistani-Americans.

"The effort to deport law-abiding people who could just as easily be allowed to continue the immigration process seriously undermines prospects for future compliance and constitutes an absurd waste of resources," the four groups said in a statement. "The mass arrests have further eroded confidence in the fairness of the INS and the immigration system among Arab and Muslim communities."

In a setback for those filing the suit, the Justice Department declared the following week that federal courts had no jurisdiction to review decisions carried out by the INS, with that power reserved only for the Supreme Court.

Anxiety Surrounding Second Round of Registration

The second INS deadline, Jan. 10, approached against this backdrop, with fear, anxiety, and anger rising in the Middle Eastern and Muslim communities. That deadline affected males from an additional 13 countries: Afghanistan, Algeria, Bahrain, Eritrea, Lebanon, Morocco, North Korea, Oman, Qatar, Somalia, Tunisia, United Arab Emirates, and Yemen. With the exception of North Korea, all are predominantly Muslim nations. This time, American Muslim groups were better prepared. The Muslim Public Affairs Council (MAPC) stationed human rights monitors at INS registration stations in 10 cities around the country. And CAIR offices across the nation provided legal referral services to those needing assistance and sponsored several "know your rights" seminars and workshops for those affected by the registration process. This time, although tensions remained high, there were no reports of widespread arrests or detentions.

Under continuous pressure from community organizations, and even from some elected officials, the INS announced a grace period for individuals from countries in the first two groups who had failed to register. These individuals were granted a second chance to register from Jan. 27 to Feb. 7.

Eventually, however, even nationals of governments supposedly "friendly" to the U.S. were included in the INS special registration program. Pakistan and Saudi Arabia were added to the list, with an initial deadline of Feb. 21, extended to

March 21. Then, citizens of staunch U.S. allies Egypt, Jordan, and Kuwait—as well as Bangladesh and Indonesia—must register by April 25 (extended from an initial deadline of March 28).

On the other hand, in an incident which dramatically demonstrated the persistent political impotence of the Arab-American and American Muslim communities, the non-Muslim nation of Armenia was also placed on the "special registration" list, but was removed less than 24 hours later, following intense lobbying by the Armenian-American community and its friends in Congress.

Amnesty International Calls for Reconsideration of Profiling

Amnesty International (AI) eventually weighed in on the controversial registration process. In a letter sent to Attorney General Ashcroft on Jan. 10 (the second deadline date), AI "expressed concern" that NSEERS "could violate United Nations and international treaties to which the U.S. is party." AI's letter went on to call upon U.S. authorities "to review its immigration laws and procedures to ensure that they are administered in accordance with international law."

AI was especially concerned about the blatant racial profiling manifested by the targeted INS registration process. "Under international standards, targeting individuals on the basis of national origin is tantamount to racial discrimination," stated Dr. William F. Schulz, executive director of Amnesty International USA (AIUSA). "We are concerned that the INS, in requiring that nationals from specific countries submit to this process, is actively engaged in racial profiling."

In its letter to Ashcroft, AI also noted that because the "special registration order applies only to immigrants from selected countries while similarly situated immigrants from other countries are not affected . . . this would appear to be in breach of the right to non-discrimination recognized under international law."

Benjamin Jealous of Amnesty's Domestic Human Rights Program commented on the irony that "those who fail to comply with the registration process face criminal charges and immediate expulsion—yet, in many cases, compliance has seemingly led to numerous rights violations. . . . It is deeply disturbing that in the U.S., following the rules can lead to denial of legal counsel, food and necessary medicine or even to physical mistreatment."

Despite widespread criticism of the special registration policy, the Justice Department and INS have shown no signs of abandoning the program, even leaving open the possibility that more countries might be added to the list in coming weeks. In the meantime, some of those due to register by spring have panicked, attempting to flee with their families to Canada. Asylum-seekers to Canada, however, have been rejected and sent back to the U.S., where out-of-status males have been detained by immigration officials upon their attempted return. As a result, entire families have been stranded in border towns, some living in their cars. In towns in Michigan, Vermont, and New York, desperate families have sought food and shelter as they await an uncertain future, many without their primary breadwinners.

Government Harassment Has Potential to Endanger Muslim Americans

These are troubled times indeed for American Muslims, Arab- and Iranian-Americans. While the surge in hate crimes against those who are or appear to be Muslim has thankfully died down, there currently is great concern among these communities about the likelihood of another misguided backlash should our nation go to war against Iraq [which occurred in March 2003]. And the continued officially sanctioned harassment of

Arabs and Muslims—citizens, immigrants, and students alike—by our own government through such policies as the INS special registration program and an array of other increasingly draconian tactics does little to alleviate the growing unease of American Muslims.

Hate Crimes Against Arabs Have Not Increased Since 9/11

Daniel Mandel

While many analysts point to statistics and firsthand accounts to make a case that Arabs have suffered increased prejudice and hostility since the terrorist attacks on September 11, others come to different conclusions. They maintain that the data are misconstrued and that the problem is overblown. Further, they question the definition of "hate crimes" by those who claim an increase of such crimes against Arabs, suggesting that the government should be very careful about using precious resources to fight a problem that does not exist.

Daniel Mandel is among those who believe that hostility toward Arabs has not increased since September 11. In the following viewpoint, he offers his perspective on what is perceived as aggressive anti-Muslim sentiment. Mandel is the director of the Zionist Organization of America's Center for Middle East Policy and associate director of the Middle East Forum in Philadelphia.

Spokesmen for Muslim groups in the West have made a large number and wide variety of claims against the societies in which they live. They speak of racism and discrimination, with the alleged misdeeds they cite ranging from defamation in the media and in Hollywood to physical attacks.

Capitol Hill and the White House seem to think these claims have a basis in fact. After the terrorist attacks of September 11, 2001, the Senate passed a resolution condemning "any acts of violence or discrimination against any Americans, including Arab Americans and American Muslims"; shortly thereafter, George W. Bush warned that intimidation of Muslims "should not and . . . will not stand in America." Presidents and Senates don't make statements of that type without believing that the situation calls for them. But does it?

Anti-Muslim Sentiment and Violence Overblown

If America were in the grip of anti-Muslim ferment, we could expect to see a major increase in hate crimes against Muslims and a corresponding lack of receptiveness to Muslim entreaties in the government, the media, and the public. According to a number of Muslim and Arab advocacy organizations, this is precisely what is happening.

The Council on American-Islamic Relations (CAIR), in "Unequal Protection," its civil-rights report for 2005, provides several graphs registering dramatic increases in reported civil-rights and hate crimes cases: 1,522 civil-rights cases in 2004, up from 1,019 in 2003 and 602 in 2002; and 141 "actual and potential" hate crimes in 2004, as against 93 in 2003 and 42 in 2002. The Arab-American Anti-Discrimination Committee (ADC) too, in its 2001–2002 report on hate crimes, alleged 165 violent incidents from January to October of 2002, amounting to a "significant increase over most years in the past decade."

The reality is rather different. Fabricated incidents and frivolous complaints have abounded in these reports and others like them. For example, no fewer than five cases of arson or vandalism of Muslim businesses appear to have been the result of attempted insurance fraud on the part of the businesses' owners. In two cases, CAIR protested on behalf of those alleging hate crimes, Mirza Akram and Amjad Abunar, demanding investigations—and then was struck dumb when each man was charged with arson. Other incidents reported by CAIR cannot be substantiated. There are no police records to back up the alleged explosion of a bomb outside a Houston mosque in July 2004. Another case CAIR cites—a mosque fire in Springfield, Mass.—was eventually ruled to be a juvenile robbery in which the fire was lit to obliterate evidence of a break-in, and was not motivated by anti-Muslim bias. Past ADC reports have referred to egg-pelting incidents against Muslims on a university campus that, on inspection, proved in one case not to have had an obvious hateful motive, and in the other to have been a fabrication by the supposed victim.

Turning to the most serious crime—murder—of eight reported by CAIR in the year following September 11, 2001, all but one had ambiguous motives and on investigation could not be attributed to anti-Muslim motivation. More recently, Daniel Pipes and Sharon Chadha took a microscope to some incidents in CAIR's latest report and concluded that, of "twenty 'anti-Muslim hate crimes' in 2004 that CAIR describes, at least six are invalid." Findings like these fatally compromise the credence that can be paid to CAIR's reports.

Outcry Against Negative Stereotypes

Beyond citing examples that appear to be outright fabrications, the authors of CAIR's reports show a remarkable ingenuity in defining what constitutes an expression of anti-Muslim bias. Hollywood has been a particular target of Muslim groups for its supposed insensitivity. The ADC decries "the extremely serious problem of negative stereotyping of Arabs and Arab Americans in the entertainment industry." With metronomic regularity, Muslim groups protest action films dealing with Middle Eastern terrorists for reinforcing a supposed culture of intolerance and racism. To Westerners, they present their argument as an appeal for fair play. Elsewhere— particularly in the Middle East—their complaint takes on an anti-Semitic complexion—the culprit now being conscienceless Jewish domination of a Hollywood that slavishly serves the interests of Israel, or of the U.S. military-industrial complex, or whatever variant thereof the subject and occasion demand.

In fact, nothing very sinister is afoot. Hollywood has always dealt in a range of stock characters and situations, and this is not reprehensible when it has a basis in fact. It is not malignity, but reality, that leads filmmakers to depict Germans as Nazis or World War II Japanese generals as imperialists. Likewise, documentaries and films on terrorism that are inspired by actual events tend to tell Middle Eastern, not Scandinavian, stories. If anything, Hollywood has latterly gone to extraordinary lengths to avoid offending Muslims, dragging other groups into service as terrorist villains. In *The Sum of All Fears*, the Middle Eastern terrorists of Tom Clancy's novel were transformed, following CAIR's intercession with the director, into European neo-Nazis. In *The Interpreter*, sub-Saharan Africans replaced the Muslims originally intended as terrorist villains. Recently, Fox acceded to CAIR's concerns over an episode of its series *24* that depicted Muslim terrorists by announcing it would give airtime to CAIR for public-service messages.

Pandering to CAIR Unnecessarily

Hollywood's pusillanimity in the face of criticism from Muslim groups mirrors a sometimes misplaced sensitivity and presumption of guilt displayed by other institutions. CAIR is a Saudi-funded organization whose founder is on record praising suicide bombers and saying he would like the Koran to be the highest authority in America, and whose personnel have been implicated in crimes consistent with these positions. One would expect that, with such a record, CAIR would be shunned. To the contrary, it is courted by government, law-enforcement agencies, civil-liberties groups, and religious bodies. Corporations too have been obsequious, perhaps because commerce is highly sensitive to organizations willing and able to trumpet claims of discrimination and insensitivity. As a result, Arabic-script logos deemed offensive to Muslims have been removed by advertisers; a broadcaster who offended

CAIR has been fired; and Internet providers have taken down websites filled with content hostile to Islam—something unlikely to occur in respect of anti-Jewish hate sites.

It is something of an Islamist triumph that such a weak case for corrective action has drawn such wide support in a country where Muslims have done exceedingly well. For the truth is that American society is generally respectful of Muslim needs and concerns. Muslim men and women who have lost their jobs for violating employer dress codes (by insisting on beards or traditional garb), or who have suffered even inadvertent discrimination in the workplace, have been either generously compensated or reinstated. Conversely, other groups suffering more from hate crimes tend to get ignored. In 2004, the FBI reported 1,374 crimes motivated by religious bias, of which 954 (67.8 percent) were committed against Jews, but only 156 (12.7 percent) against Muslims. This has not resulted in allegations of an anti-Jewish crime wave in the United States, much less in concerted action to address pervasive racism against Jews.

On any serious index of hate crimes and discrimination against Muslims, Americans are not significantly represented. We should remember this truth next time complaints emerge from CAIR and likeminded groups. In particular, the mainstream media should treat these claims without credulity and independently verify allegations; government and institutions should shun radical pressure groups; and corporations, perhaps the most vulnerable target of campaigns alleging racism and insensitivity, should deploy strategies other than caving in.

Chronology

1500s
First African slaves arrive in America.

September 9, 1739
The Stono slave rebellion begins with twenty participants, but its number grows to an estimated one hundred.

1800
Gabriel Prosser, a Virginia slave, and others are hanged for planning a revolt in Richmond.

1820
Missouri Compromise prohibits slavery north of Missouri.

August 22, 1831
Nat Turner's slave rebellion erupts in Southampton, Virginia.

1833
Free African Americans and whites found the American Anti-Slavery Society.

1857
U.S. Supreme Court hands down decision in *Dred Scott v. Sanford.*

October 1859
John Brown and his followers raid federal arsenal at Harpers Ferry, Virginia.

January 1863
U.S. president Abraham Lincoln issues the Emancipation Proclamation.

December 1865

The Thirteenth Amendment is ratified, abolishing slavery.

April 1866

The Civil Rights Act is passed by Congress, giving black citizens civil rights equal to those of whites.

December 29, 1890

Lakota Sioux are massacred at Wounded Knee.

1892

Ida B. Wells publishes *Southern Horrors: Lynch Law in All Its Phases*.

1895

Ida B. Wells publishes *A Red Record*, describing her antilynching efforts.

1909

Lynching and other attacks by whites in black neighborhoods in Illinois lead to the establishment of the National Association for the Advancement of Colored People (NAACP).

1930

W.D. Fard founds the Black Muslims.

1934

Elijah Muhammad succeeds W.D. Fard in leading the Black Muslims.

August 1955

A fourteen-year-old African American boy named Emmett Till is tortured and murdered by at least two white men.

1963

Mississippi NAACP leader Medgar Evers is assassinated.

September 1963

Four African American children are killed when a black church in Birmingham, Alabama, is bombed

July 1964

Ku Klux Klan guns down Lemuel Penn on a road in Georgia.

August 1964

The bodies of murdered civil rights workers James Chaney, Michael Schwerner, and Andrew Goodman are found.

February 21, 1965

Malcolm X is assassinated.

August 1965

Race riots break out in Watts, Los Angeles, after police arrest and beat a black man suspected of drunk driving.

1966

The Black Panther Party is established in Oakland, California, by Huey Newton and Bobby Seale.

April 4, 1968

Martin Luther King Jr. is assassinated.

1970

Twenty-three-year-old African American Henry Marrow Jr. is killed because of his race in Oxford, North Carolina.

1971

A Wilmington grocery store owned by a white man is fire-bombed by the "Wilmington 10," nine African American men and a white woman. They are convicted, but the convictions are overturned in 1980.

1979

The first state hate-crime law is passed by Massachusetts.

1981

The Anti-Defamation League outlines model legislation aimed at hate crimes.

1982

Chinese American Vincent Chin is bludgeoned to death with a baseball bat in Michigan.

1983

The U.S. Civil Rights Commission calls for research on hate crimes.

1985

Congress has its first hearing on hate crime.

1990

The Hate Crimes Statistics Act is signed into law.

1991

Rodney King, an African American, is beaten by Los Angeles police. The beating is captured on videotape and widely broadcast. The acquittal of the police officers one year later sparks riots in predominantly black neighborhoods in Los Angeles.

August 15, 1992

Vietnamese American student Luyen Phan Nguyen is beaten to death by a group of white men shouting racial epithets. Three men receive prison sentences.

August 14, 1993

Cambodian Americans Sophy Soeung and Nhang Nhem are brutally attacked by a group of white men shouting out racial slurs. Nhem dies from his injuries, and one attacker receives a life sentence.

October 2, 1993

The Japanese American Citizens League office in Sacramento, California, is firebombed by the Aryan Liberation Front. There are no injuries, only property damage.

1994

The Hate Crime Sentencing Enhancement Act is enacted, calling for harsher penalties for federal hate crimes.

1995

The Asian Pacific Legal Consortium releases a study indicating that violence against Asians in Southern California has increased significantly over the past year.

June 18, 1995

Thanh Mai and two other Vietnamese Americans are attacked in a nightclub by three white men invoking racial slurs. Mai is killed, but his attacker only receives a manslaughter sentence; hate crime laws are not applied.

November 8, 1995

Robert Page of Novato, California, tells police he wanted to kill a "Chinaman" as an explanation for killing Eddy Wu. He is sentenced to eleven years in prison.

1996

The first Internet hate crime is prosecuted after undergraduate student Richard Machado sends around an e-mail slandering and threatening Asian American students.

1997–2003

The Hate Crimes Prevention Act is put before Congress three times (1997, 1999, 2003) but does not pass.

June 7, 1998

The nation mourns the murder of James Byrd Jr., an African American man who was beaten and dragged to death behind a truck by three white men in Texas.

October 7, 1998

Matthew Shepard, a young gay man, is brutally attacked and abandoned by two men in Wyoming. He dies five days later.

July 1999

Twenty-one-year-old Benjamin Smith goes on a hate-motivated shooting spree, injuring six Jews and three African Americans and killing a Korean student and an African American before turning the gun on himself.

September 11, 2001

Terrorists attack the United States by flying passenger planes into the New York World Trade Center and the Pentagon. A fourth plane crashed in Pennsylvania before reaching its target.

May 3, 2007

The U.S. House of Representatives passes the Law Enforcement Hate Crimes Prevention Act to expand the prosecution of bias-motivated crimes. The Senate considers the analogous Matthew Shepard Act.

Organizations to Contact

The editors compiled the following list of organizations concerned with the topics discussed in this book. The descriptions are from materials provided by the organizations. All have information available for interested readers. The list was compiled just prior to publication of the present volume; the information provided here may change. Be aware that many organizations take several weeks or longer to respond to inquiries, so allow as much time as possible.

American Civil Liberties Union (ACLU)
125 Broad St., 18th Floor, New York, NY   10004
Web site: www.aclu.org

The ACLU is a national organization that works to defend Americans' civil rights as guaranteed in the U.S. Constitution. The ACLU publishes the semiannual newsletter *Civil Liberties Alert* as well as briefing papers, including "Hate Speech on Campus" and "Racial Justice."

Anti-Defamation League (ADL)
PO Box 96226, Washington, DC   20090-6226
(202) 452-8310
e-mail: washington-dc@adl.org
Web site: www.adl.org

The ADL is an international organization that fights prejudice and extremism. It collects, organizes, and distributes information about anti-Semitism, hate crimes, bigotry, and racism, and also monitors hate groups and extremists on the Internet. Among its many publications are the reports *Explosion of Hate: The Growing Danger of the National Alliance, Danger: Extremism—the Major Vehicles and Voices on America's Far Right Fringe*, and *Hate on the World Wide Web*.

Center for Democratic Renewal
PO Box 50469, Atlanta, GA   30302
(404) 221-0025 • fax: (404) 221-0045
Web site: www.thecdr.org

Formerly known as the National Anti-Klan Network, this nonprofit organization monitors hate-group activity and white supremacist activity in America and opposes bias-motivated violence. It publishes the bimonthly *Monitor* magazine, the report *The Fourth Wave: A Continuing Conspiracy to Burn Black Churches*, and the book *When Hate Groups Come to Town*.

Center for Women Policy Studies
1776 Massachusetts Ave. NW, Suite 450
Washington, DC   20036
(202) 872-1770 • fax: (202) 296-8962
e-mail: cwps@centerwomenpolicy.org
Web site: www.centerwomenpolicy.org

The Center for Women Policy Studies' goal is to shape public policy to improve women's lives and preserve women's human rights. The center has released numerous reports and studies over the years analyzing the effects on women of poverty, HIV/AIDS, reproductive rights and health, violence, workplace diversity, disabilities, and more.

Gay & Lesbian Alliance Against Defamation (GLAAD)
5455 Wilshire Blvd., #1500, Los Angeles, CA   90036
(323) 933-2240 • fax: (323) 933-2241
Web site: www.glaad.org

The Gay & Lesbian Alliance Against Defamation is dedicated to promoting and ensuring fair, accurate, and inclusive representation of people and events in the media as a means of eliminating homophobia and discrimination based on gender identity and sexual orientation. Through campaigns, meetings with policy makers, interaction with the media, and mobilization of grassroots efforts, GLAAD has grown in its reach and influence. Among its publications are topical articles, brochures, and training manuals addressing research and issues of the day as well as the *GLAAD Media Reference Guide*.

National Association for the Advancement of Colored People (NAACP)

4805 Mt. Hope Dr., Baltimore, MD   21215
(877) NAACP-98 • fax: (202) 463-2953
e-mail: washingtonbureau@naacpnet.org
Web site: www.naacp.org

The NAACP aims to ensure the political, educational, social, and economic equality of rights of all persons and to eliminate racial hatred and discrimination. In pursuit of these goals, the NAACP is vocal and active in the media and with government officials and representatives, seeking to influence legislation and public policy. The NAACP publishes the magazine *Crisis* as well as a variety of newsletters, books, and pamphlets addressing topics ranging from legal issues to education.

National Gay and Lesbian Task Force

1325 Massachusetts Ave. NW, Suite 600
Washington, DC   20005
(202) 393-5177 • fax: (202) 393-2241
e-mail: thetaskforce@thetaskforce.org
Web site: www.thetaskforce.org

The National Gay and Lesbian Task Force's goal is to build the grassroots power of the lesbian, gay, bisexual, and transgender (LGBT) community by training activists and equipping state and local organizations with the skills needed to organize broad-based campaigns to defeat anti-LGBT referenda and advance pro-LGBT legislation. Numerous reports and studies have been authored by the institute, addressing such issues as tax expenditures, health services, and hate crime.

National Youth Violence Prevention Resource Center (NYVPRC)

PO Box 10809, Rockville, MD 20849-0809
1-866-SAFEYOUTH • fax: (301) 562-1001
e-mail: nyvprc@safeyouth.org
Web site: www.safeyouth.org

Partnered with various federal agencies, the NYVPRC offers the latest tools to facilitate discussion with children in order to resolve conflicts nonviolently, to stop bullying, to prevent teen suicide, and to end violence committed by and against young people. It provides publications, posters, brochures, manuals, reports, fact sheets, and other materials for schools and individuals, all at no charge. The center also generates reports for Congress on issues such as teen violence.

Southern Poverty Law Center (SPLC)

400 Washington Ave., Montgomery, AL 36104
(334) 956-8200 • fax: (334) 956-8488
e-mail: info@splcenter.org
Web site: www.splcenter.org

The SPLC is a globally influential organization known for its watchful eye on hate groups and its commitment to teaching tolerance. Staff members regularly conduct training sessions for police, schools, and civil rights and community groups, and they often serve as experts at hearings and conferences. The center's publications include *Intelligence Report* and *Teaching Tolerance*.

For Further Research

Books

Anti-Defamation League, *Hate Crimes Statutes: A Response to Anti-Semitism, Vandalism and Violent Bigotry.* New York: Anti-Defamation League of B'nai B'rith, 1991.

W. Fitzhugh Brundage, *Lynching in the New South: Georgia and Virginia, 1880–1930.* Urbana: University of Illinois Press, 1993.

Sara Bullard, *The Ku Klux Klan: A History of Racism and Violence.* Montgomery, AL: Southern Poverty Law Center, 1988.

David M. Chalmers, *Hooded Americanism: The History of the Ku Klux Klan.* Durham, NC: Duke University Press, 1987.

Chan Sucheng, ed., *Entry Denied: Exclusion and the Chinese Community in America, 1882–1943.* Philadelphia: Temple University Press, 1991.

Gary Comstock, *Violence Against Lesbians and Gay Men.* New York: Columbia University Press, 1991.

Henry Friedlander, *The Origins of Nazi Genocide: From Euthanasia to the Final Solution.* Chapel Hill: University of North Carolina Press, 1995.

Eugene D. Genovese, *From Rebellion to Revolution: Afro-American Slave Revolts in the Making of the Modern World.* Baton Rouge: Louisiana State University Press, 1979.

Mark S. Hamm, *American Skinheads: The Criminology and Control of Hate Crime.* Westport, CT: Praeger, 1994.

Gregory M. Herek and Kevin Berrill, eds., *Hate Crimes: Confronting Violence Against Lesbians and Gay Men.* Newbury Park, CA: Sage, 1992.

James B. Jacobs and Kimberly Potter, *Hate Crimes: Criminal Law and Identity Politics.* Oxford, UK: Oxford University Press, 2001.

Robert J. Kelly and Jess Maghan, eds., *Hate Crime: The Global Politics of Polarization.* Carbondale: Southern Illinois University Press, 1998.

Roger Lane, *Roots of Violence in Black Philadelphia, 1860–1900.* Cambridge, MA: Harvard University Press, 1986.

Leon F. Litwack, *Been in the Storm So Long: The Aftermath of Slavery.* New York: Knopf, 1979.

Charles J. McClain, *In Search of Equality: The Chinese Struggle Against Discrimination in Nineteenth-Century America.* Berkeley and Los Angeles: University of California Press, 1994.

Barbara Perry, *In the Name of Hate: Understanding Hate Crimes.* New York: Routledge, 2001.

Howard N. Rabinowitz, *Race Relations in the Urban South, 1865–1890.* Athens: University of Georgia Press, 1996.

Michael R. Ronczkowski, *Terrorism and Organized Hate Crime: Intelligence Gathering, Analysis, and Investigations.* Boca Raton, FL: CRC Press, 2004.

Carl Sandburg, *The Chicago Race Riots, July 1919.* New York: Harcourt, 1969.

Herbert D. Shapiro, *White Violence and Black Response: From Reconstruction to Montgomery.* Amherst: University of Massachusetts Press, 1988.

Joseph P. Shapiro, *No Pity: People with Disabilities Forging a New Civil Rights Movement.* New York: Random House, 1993.

Franklin E. Zimring, *American Youth Violence*. New York: Oxford University Press, 1998.

Periodicals

James F. Anderson and Willie Brooks Jr., "Preventing Hate Crime and Profiling Hate Crime Offenders," *Western Journal of Black Studies*, vol. 26, no. 3, 2002.

Harold Baron, "Black Powerlessness in Chicago," *Transaction*, November 1968.

David Boesel et al., "White Institutions and Black Rage," *Transaction*, March 1969.

James C. Clark, "Civil Rights Leader Harry T. Moore and the Ku Klux Klan in Florida," *Florida Historical Quarterly*, October 1994.

Harold Cruse, "Revolutionary Nationalism and the Afro-American," *Studies on the Left*, vol. 2, 1962.

Carl N. Degler, "Racism in the United States: An Essay Review," *Journal of Southern History*, February 1972.

Bruce Fein and Brian Levin, "Does America Need a Federal Hate-Crime Law?" *Insight on the News*, November 23, 1998.

Joseph Fernandez, "Bringing Hate Crimes into Focus," *Harvard Civil Rights/Civil Liberties Law Review*, vol. 26, 1991.

James A. Gondles, Jr. "Hate Crime: Not New, but Still Alarming," *Corrections Today*, August 1999.

Donald P. Green, Laurence H. McFalls, and Jennifer K. Smith, "Hate Crime: An Emergent Research Agenda," *Annual Review of Sociology*, 2001.

Delinda C. Hanley, "In the Wake of 9-11 President Bush and Muslim Leaders Work to Protect Muslim Americans," *Washington Report on Middle East Affairs*, November 2001.

Gregory M. Herek, "Hate Crimes Against Lesbians and Gay Men: Issues for Research and Policy," *American Psychologist*, vol. 44, 1989.

Tanya Kateri Hernandez, "Bias Crimes: Unconscious Racism in the Prosecution of Racially-Motivated Violence," *Yale Law Journal*, vol. 99, 1990.

James B. Jacobs, "Should Hate Be a Crime?" *Public Interest*, Fall 1993.

Valerie Jenness and Ryken Grattet, "The Criminalization of Hate: A Comparison of Structural and Polity Influences on the Passage of 'Bias-Crime' Legislation in the United States," *Sociological Perspectives*, vol. 39, 1996.

Harold Kennedy, "Cussed and Robbed, Shot and Boycotted," *Birmingham (AL) News Magazine*, June 7, 1970.

Jabez A. Langley, "Garveyism and African Nationalism," *Race*, October 1969.

Erika Lee, "Echoes of the Chinese Exclusion Era in Post-9/11 America," *Chinese America: History and Perspectives*, 2005.

Brian Levin, "Violence Against Women: Is It a Hate Crime?" *Klanwatch Intelligence Report*, June 1994.

Donna Minkowitz, "Love and Hate in Laramie: Matthew Shepard Was Killed in Wyoming's Most Progressive Town," *Nation*, July 12, 1999.

Paul Rogers, "Anti-Bias Law Spurs No Action," *San Jose (CA) Mercury News*, May 1992.

Dennis Shepard, "My Son Matt," *Advocate*, April 30, 2000.

Andrew Sullivan, "What's So Bad About Hate?" *New York Times Magazine*, September 26, 1999.

Eric Tischler, "Can Tolerance Be Taught?" *Corrections Today*, August 1999.

Index